GO **Wild** WITH QUILTS

Margaret Rolfe

Fourteen North American Birds and Animals

That Patchwork Place®

ACKNOWLEDGMENTS

Many people helped to make this book a reality, so I would like to thank Kathy Burkey, Heather and John Campbell, Marjorie Coleman, Barbara Goddard, Ann Haddad, Beryl Hodges, Lyn Inall, Donna Sunderland, and Judy Turner, for all the ways in which they helped. Special thanks to Lee Cleland, Beth Miller, and Elizabeth Rose for their immaculate quilting. I am grateful to Jan Laut for her help with the Swallow design. My parents, Linda and Alex Poppins, gave their help and support, as always. Phil, my younger son, has illustrated the animals with superb drawings and has been my "quality-control monitor" for the designs and the quilts; his contribution is incalculable. Bernie, my older son, and Melinda, my daughter, gave me much practical assistance and were very tolerant of a preoccupied mother. I must give special thanks to Nancy Cameron Armstrong, for her inspiration to make the book in the first place and for always believing in it. And throughout everything, I am deeply indebted to my husband, Barry, who believes in me and who always turns my "I can't" into "I can."

Dedication
To Nancy Cameron Armstrong

CREDITS

Editors . . . . Ursula Reikes
                                                 Barbara Weiland
Copy Editor . . . . Liz McGehee
Managing Editor . . . . Greg Sharp
Text Design . . . . Stephanie Benson

Cover Design . . . . Chris Christiansen
Typesetting . . . . ArtWorks
Photography . . . . Brent Kane
                                                 Mike Fisher
Illustration and Graphics . . . . . Karin LaFramboise
Wildlife Illustrations . . . . Phil Rolfe

Go Wild with Quilts:
14 North American Birds and Animals ©
© 1993 by Margaret Rolfe

That Patchwork Place, Inc.,
PO Box 118, Bothell, WA 98041-0118
USA

Printed in Hong Kong
99 98 97 96 95 94 93   9 8 7 6 5 4 3

Library of Congress Cataloging-in-Publication Data

Rolfe, Margaret.
      Go wild with quilts: 14 North American birds and animals / Margaret Rolfe.
          p.   cm.
      ISBN 1-56477-019-2 :
      1. Patchwork — Patterns. 2. Quilting — Patterns.
3. Decoration and ornament — Animal forms — Canada.
4. Decoration and ornament — Animal forms — United States.   I. Title.
TT835.R6512   1993
746.9'7 — dc20   93-9765
                                                            CIP

CONTENTS

INTRODUCTION

Images of animals are the oldest known pictures in human art and appear in myriad artistic forms throughout the centuries. To make an image is a uniquely human characteristic, and we derive inspiration constantly from the beauty of nature around us. As quilters, we find it natural to extend images of animals into the medium of quilts.

In the late twentieth century, we are becoming more aware of our place within the environment. A respect for nature and the animals and birds that share our planet is essential if our own species is to survive.

Animals and birds have been part of my quilts from the first ones I made using my own designs ten years ago. Australian animals and birds were my starting point, and I created both appliqué and pieced designs. I found myself increasingly intrigued by the challenge of pieced designs. I wanted my animals and birds to have a feeling of life, so I did not want to be restricted solely to the traditional shapes of squares and triangles. Yet, I also did not want to make designs that were difficult to sew—I don't enjoy sewing around corners. So I invented what I have come to call straight-line patchwork, which simply means that my blocks have been designed so that all seams are sewn in a straight line, provided you follow the suggested piecing order.

Straight-line piecing gives me "the freedom of the block," so to speak. All kinds of shapes, large and small with many or few sides, can be used, but they all fit together neatly with straight seams.

From Australian animals, it seemed natural to go on to make other animal designs. North America has been a second home for me. I spent nearly five happy years in Canada and have lived for many months in the United States, returning to visit regularly. As a result, I was inspired to create this set of designs for North American birds and animals. While I was working in an office in Toronto, I watched the blue jays out on a fence nearby. I also delighted in the busy squirrels in the parks and along elm-lined streets. Of course, animals know no political boundaries, and some of the same animals and birds are found in Europe and even in Australia.

While I enjoy creating new block designs, I continue to love the traditional ones. The quilts in this book combine animal designs with traditional patterns. Each animal block includes an example for its use, but these represent only a few of the many possibilities. I hope you will use these animal block designs to come up with lots of ideas and create your own quilts. Above all, enjoy yourself!

Margaret Rolfe

MATERIALS AND EQUIPMENT

Fabrics

Today, there is a wonderful selection of 100% cotton fabrics in a rainbow of colors made especially for quilters. Pure cotton washes easily, cuts cleanly, sews without stretching, and presses crisp and flat. Sometimes, however, you may want a special color or print that is only available in a blend or man-made fiber. There are also many marvelous decorator fabrics available with enticing colors and prints. Since color and pattern are more important than anything else, go ahead and use these fabrics as necessary, but be aware that they may be more difficult to handle. Prewash and press all fabrics before use. Make a habit of washing all fabrics immediately after purchase—it's worth the trouble. Fabric requirements in this book are based on 40 usable inches after preshrinking. Because of the various sizes required for piecing, yardage requirements of ⅛ yard and ¼ yard may be ample, and sometimes you may have fabric left over.

Batting

Different varieties and thicknesses of batting abound, and you should choose what you find most comfortable to sew. A thinner batting is ideal for machine quilting.

Thread

For machine piecing, use a white dressmaking or serging thread. Use a dark thread only where the fabrics are predominantly dark.

For hand piecing, match the thread to the fabrics you are stitching.

For hand quilting, use a quilting thread. There is a variety of colors from which to choose besides traditional white.

For machine quilting, use one of the following:

Dressmaking thread to match, blend, or contrast with the color of the fabrics.

Clear, monofilament thread (on the top of the

machine only, not in the bobbin) that will blend into all colors. This monofilament thread also comes in a dark shade to use with dark fabrics.

For embroidery, use embroidery floss, which comes in a variety of colors. Some of the details on the animals, such as eyes and feet, are added with simple embroidery.

Template Materials

There are two choices for making templates, either cardboard or template plastic.

1. For cardboard templates, use large sheets of cardboard. If you are drawing the block yourself, you also need large sheets of graph paper, preferably marked in ¼" divisions. A glue stick is essential to adhere either the photocopy or drawing of the block to the cardboard. Do not use other kinds of paste or glue; they are too wet and cause stretching and distortion.
2. For plastic templates, purchase template plastic from quilt shops. Trace the drawn or photocopied block onto the plastic with a pencil or fine permanent marking pen. Template plastic with a grid marked on it is useful if you are drawing the block yourself, since you can draw the block directly onto the template plastic.

Drawing Equipment

If you are drawing the blocks and making cardboard templates, you need pencils, an eraser, a small set of colored pencils, and a ruler. For plastic templates, you need a fine permanent marking pen.

To mark light fabric, use a soft pencil, such as a #2, or use a light-colored pencil (silver, yellow, or white) for dark fabrics.

For marking quilting designs on a quilt top, draw lightly with a #2 pencil or use dressmaking chalk. Keep all your pencils sharp with a good-quality pencil sharpener. Scotch™ tape and masking tape are also useful in quiltmaking, so keep these handy.

Photocopier

The animal blocks can be easily enlarged on a photocopier if you do not want to draw the block yourself. Photocopying may be done at copying centers and some libraries for a small fee.

Sandpaper Board

A sheet of fine sandpaper, carefully glued to a thin piece of particle board, is very useful for marking fabrics. The sandpaper grabs the fabric and stops it from slipping as you mark. You can sit down in your favorite armchair, put your sandpaper board on your lap, and mark your fabrics in comfort. Alternatively, use some Scotch tape to attach a sheet of fine sandpaper to a table top and mark on top of this.

Scissors and Shears

Good-quality dressmaking shears make cutting pleasant and easy. You also need paper scissors for cutting cardboard or plastic for your templates. Small, sharp, pointed scissors are useful for appliqué.

Rotary Cutter and Mat

The rotary cutter and mat have revolutionized modern quiltmaking, simplifying the cutting of strips and simple geometric shapes, such as squares, triangles, and rectangles.

Quilters' Rulers

To go with your rotary cutter and mat, you need a special long quilters' ruler, which is made of clear acrylic with accurate markings across its length and width. A 6" or 8" Bias Square® cutting guide and a large square ruler (12" x 12") are also useful. A ¼"-wide strip of plastic is helpful for marking ¼"-wide seam allowances onto template shapes. Use a right triangle to mark 45° angles.

Layout Board

It is essential to lay out the straight-line patchwork animal block before you begin piecing so that each piece in the design is correctly oriented toward its neighbors. Make a permanent layout board by gluing white felt to a 20" square of cardboard. You can also use this handy board to lay out all the pieces of traditional blocks. (Even with classic blocks like the Ohio Star, it is essential to get those triangles the right way around, and the best way to do this is to lay out the block in front of you.) Alternatively, you can lay out your blocks on a 20" square of paper (not newspaper—it rips too easily), or for traveling, you can lay out and pin your block to a 20" square of felt, which can be rolled or folded.

Pins

For piecing, glass- or plastic-headed pins are easy to use and easy to find when you drop them.

For machine quilting, use safety pins (approximately 1" in length) to hold the layers together as you quilt.

Needles

For hand piecing, use a needle that you find comfortable.

For hand quilting, use a "between" needle, in a size that suits you.

For appliqué, use a fine crewel needle.

For embroidery, use a crewel needle that will

take two or three strands of embroidery floss.

Sewing Machine

The most fundamental tool for modern patchwork is the sewing machine. Lots of fancy stitches are not needed, but a couple of features are desirable for quiltmaking: the ability to move the needle left and right (to make an exact ¼"-wide seam when the fabric is lined up against the edge of the presser foot) and a walking foot, which makes machine quilting much easier.

Ironing Board

If you have the space, set up your ironing board next to your machine or make a small, portable ironing board by wrapping several layers of cardboard with an old towel, then covering the whole thing with muslin. Put this on a chair next to your sewing machine so that you can sew and press without having to get up each time you need the iron. This makes piecing much easier.

Iron

An iron is used constantly for machine piecing, as each seam must be pressed before any cross seams are sewn. A spray container of water next to the iron is useful for dampening stubborn pieces.

Thimbles

Wear a well-fitting thimble to protect your finger while hand quilting. You might also want to protect the finger that guides the quilting stitch underneath by wearing another thimble or finger protector.

Quilting Hoop

A quilting hoop holds the three layers of a quilt smoothly in place while you are hand quilting. Choose a size that is comfortable for you.

PIECING the ANIMAL BLOCKS

Quilts in this book combine two types of blocks: straight-line patchwork animal blocks and traditional patchwork blocks. Different methods are used for piecing these two kinds of blocks, so it is very important that you understand the differences and use the method appropriate for the block you are making.

Straight-Line Patchwork

This book offers a set of new and different patchwork block designs for making animals and birds. All kinds of oddly shaped geometric pieces are used to create the animal blocks.

These are the shapes for the bear.

The blocks are easy to sew, however, because all pieces are sewn together with straight seams. It is these straight seams that give the name to this technique: straight-line patchwork.

The majority of traditional patchwork patterns are made up of combinations of squares, rectangles, and triangles. In making animal designs, I wanted to use shapes that were different from these traditional shapes, yet I did not want to create blocks

that were difficult to machine piece. Previously, animal designs were either created by using multitudes of little squares and triangles (so that each block had an enormous number of pieces), or by having lots of odd shapes, which meant sewing around many inset corners (making piecing difficult). I wanted to avoid both of these options. My aim always is to make patchwork designs that are as simple as possible and I use only straight seams. My guides to simplicity are the Shoo Fly block, which has thirteen pieces, and the Ohio Star, which has twenty-one pieces. I try to have the number of pieces in my straight-line blocks somewhere between these two. The bear, for instance, has only fifteen pieces. I don't always succeed in creating a block with less than twenty-one pieces, because some animals need more pieces to give them their true character. But all of my blocks have less than forty-five pieces, the number in a traditional Bear's Paw block.

Straight-line patchwork is especially practical for machine sewing, where previously sewn seams are sewn down when additional pieces are added. Straight-line patchwork is not essential for hand piecing, because seam allowances are not sewn down, but it still makes for easier construction and sewing.

The concept behind straight-line patchwork is simple and not really original. It is the same con-

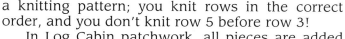

cept that underlies the method for making a Log Cabin block. By adding the Log Cabin pieces one at a time in a certain order, you sew only straight seams, and what at first glance seems complex, is, in fact, simple.

Like any technique, straight-line patchwork has its own rules.

Rule Number 1. Follow the piecing order. To make the piecing order understandable, each piece in the block is numbered.

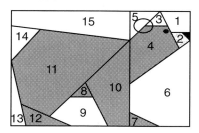

The plus sign always indicates a seam. When the piecing order says 1 + 2, pick up pieces 1 and 2 and sew them together. Once joined together, the pieces become a unit, which is signified by putting the numbers into parentheses and placing a dash between the numbers, so that the unit created by sewing 1 and 2 together becomes (1-2).

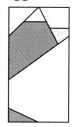

1 + 2 means to sew pieces 1 and 2 together.

Once sewn, the pieces are a unit called (1-2).

The piecing order is given as a series of lettered steps, which look like this:
A. 1 + 2
B. 3 + 4
C. (1-2) + (3-4) + 5

These are the first three steps in putting the Bear block together. First, you join pieces 1 and 2 together; second, you join pieces 3 and 4 together; and third, you join together the units you have just created, units (1-2) and (3-4), to piece 5. You have now created a new unit, which in the next step will be called (1-5) because it comprises all the pieces from 1 through 5.

Each step is lettered so you know exactly where you are and represents a seam (or number of seams) that can be sewn without crossing another seam. Following the piecing order is much like following

a knitting pattern; you knit rows in the correct order, and you don't knit row 5 before row 3!

In Log Cabin patchwork, all pieces are added onto the existing unit. In straight-line patchwork, pieces are sewn together into units that may be temporarily set aside while another unit is being sewn. Completed units are then sewn together into a larger unit or section.

Sections are indicated in the piecing order by a line of squiggles.

When you see this line of squiggles, you know that you have completed one section of the design.

Rule Number 2. Lay out the block, with each piece in its correct position, before you begin to sew. This will help you determine which sides of the pieces should be sewn together.

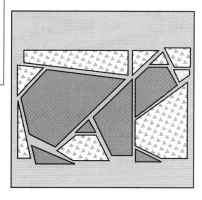

Rule Number 3. Mark seam lines and do not automatically add seam allowances. There is a good reason for this, which you will discover when you actually sew two pieces together. The odd shapes in straight-line patchwork do not sit neatly on top of each other, with corners accurately matched like two squares or two identical triangles do. Seam lines are marked so that pieces will match up correctly at the corners. In fact, it is similar to the procedure for hand piecing except the sewing can be done by machine.

Please read this even if you read nothing else!

The important rules to note about straight-line patchwork are:
1. Follow the piecing order.
2. Lay out the block before you begin to sew.
3. Mark all seam lines.
4. Cut ⅜"-wide seam allowances for most pieces and ½"-wide seam allowances for small or long, pointed pieces.

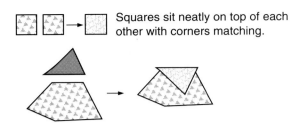

Squares sit neatly on top of each other with corners matching.

The odd shapes in straight-line patchwork will not match at the corners unless seam lines are marked.

Rule Number 4. Use ⅜" to ½" seam allowances, adding them as you cut around the marked shapes, especially for small pieces and long, narrow, pointed pieces. There are usually a few of these small or narrow pieces in each design. I suggest cutting a ⅜"-wide seam allowance on most pieces and a full ½"-wide seam allowance on small and long, pointed pieces. The wide seam allowances give you more fabric with which to pin and stitch, and the pieces are less likely to move as you sew. I strongly recommend that you do not mark a ¼" cutting line outside your marked seam line. This adds an unnecessary, time-consuming step. Trim excess fabric from the wider seam allowances after the seam is sewn, to make the back of the patchwork neat as well as to eliminate unnecessary bulk. Just remember the rule: small pieces—large seam allowances, and you won't have any trouble.

All of this is easier to do than to describe, so I urge you to try a block, such as the Bear block. A complete step-by-step diagram for piecing the Bear block is given on page 25, and this would be a good place to start. As soon as you actually follow the system, you will see how easy and logical it is. I am told constantly, "Your designs just go together!"

Making Templates

Templates for straight-line patchwork are always accurate because you draw or photocopy the whole block. Any changes to the original block (whether by accident or intentional) will not result in inaccurate templates, because when the drawn or photocopied block is cut up, it will go back together perfectly.

All the designs are shown on a grid of squares, indicated by dashed lines. By changing the size of the squares, you can enlarge the design to whatever size you need. For example, if the design is drawn on a grid of 8 x 8 squares and you make each square 1¼", the finished block will be 10" x 10". If you make each square 1½", the finished block will be 12" x 12".

The designs can be enlarged by drawing or photocopying.

To Draw the Block Design:

1. Choose a finished block size from the size options given with each design. Using graph paper or template plastic, draw the same number of squares in the desired size.

    Example: The bear pattern is drawn on a grid of 8 x 12 squares. To make a bear, 6" x 9", make each square ¾". Alternatively, to make an 8" x 12" bear, make each square 1".

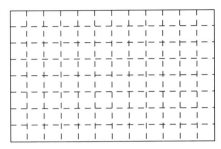

Use a different-colored pencil or pen for drawing the grid squares from the one you use to draw the lines of the design, so that you can distinguish the difference between grid lines and the design lines that create the animal shapes.

2. Use a pencil (or pen on template plastic) to draw the design onto the grid, using the grid to locate where the lines should be placed. Draw the longest lines first. It is easy to draw the lines if you first mark the ends of each line with a dot, then join the dots.

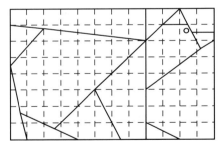

3. Mark each piece with its correct number.
4. Color or sketch a pattern onto the pieces, to help identify which pieces go with which fabrics.

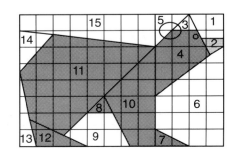

If you are coloring the pieces, use the same colors that you will be using in the quilt. For example, in coloring the bear, use black for all the pieces that will be black, and brown for the muzzle. The background can be colored or left as is.

Alternatively, you can sketch in a pattern instead of using color. For the Bear block, sketch a diagonal stripe on all the pieces that will be black, use dots on the muzzle piece, and leave the background unpatterned. Throughout this book, you can see how patterns and shading are used to identify shapes in the block designs.

To Photocopy the Block Design:

Yes, it is OK to photocopy the designs in this book for your own personal use! Usually, this is not recommended for making templates, because the process of photocopying distorts the templates slightly. The small distortions in one shape can add up to larger distortions when several shapes that have been photocopied are repeated or combined. But with the straight-line patchwork animal blocks, the whole block is being copied and therefore any distortions affect the whole block and do not change the accuracy of the final templates. You will find, however, that the outside edge of an enlarged pattern will not be totally accurate, so you will need to make some slight adjustments at the sides.

1. Choose the size of block you need for your quilt. The size of each design, as it is presented on the pages of this book, is printed below the design. For example, the bear design is 4" x 6". Below each design is a list of sizes and the percentage enlargements required to make them. To make the Bear block 6" x 9", you need to enlarge the original design by 150%; to make it 8" x 12", enlarge the original design by 200%.

    Percentages for enlargements are given for each block. If you are not mathematical, skip to step 2. But for those who want to work out the percentages themselves, here is how to do it:

    a) Subtract the size of the original block as it appears on the page from the desired size. For example, to enlarge the bear from a 4" x 6" block to a 6" x 9" block, subtract the original width of 6" from the desired width of 9"; the result is 3.

    You can use either length or width measurements for your calculations. Subtracting 4 from 6 will yield the same end result. But you must use both length measurements or both width measurements; you cannot mix length and width measurements.

    b) Find out what proportion the resultant number is of the original width; 3 is half of 6.

c) Turn the "half" into a percentage and add 100. To complete our example, the half becomes 50%, and when added to 100, becomes 150%. So, to enlarge the bear from 4" x 6" to 6" x 9", enlarge the design by 150%.

    Here is another example. You need the Bear block to be 10" wide. Subtract 6 (the original width) from 10; the result is 4, which is ⅔ of 6. Turn the ⅔ into a percentage, which is 67% (it is actually 66.6666%, but the figure 67% is used for convenience). Add 100, and the enlargement percentage is 167%.

    Since many photocopiers can only enlarge up to 150%, enlargements greater than 150% must be done in two or more steps. In this situation, the percentages must be worked out for each step and will not be the same. To increase the Bear block from 4" x 6" to 8" x 12", first enlarge the design by 150% (4" x 6" to 6" x 9"). Then take the enlarged design and enlarge it again by 133% (6" x 9" to 8" x 12").

    Percentages for different-sized blocks have already been calculated and are provided with each block. If you wish to make a block in a size other than those listed, you will need to calculate the percentage yourself, as directed above.

2. Select the largest size of paper available on the photocopier. Some designs may not fit onto the largest-sized paper, and you will need to make two copies, one of the top of the design and one of the bottom. Tape or glue the two parts together to make the whole design.

3. Set the photocopier to the enlargement size you need, as specified for each design. Remember, some photocopiers only enlarge up to 150%, in which case you may need to enlarge a design in two or more steps.

4. Measure the photocopied design, and with a ruler and pencil, adjust the sides in or out as necessary to make the block exactly the size you need. Such alterations will not substantially change the design.

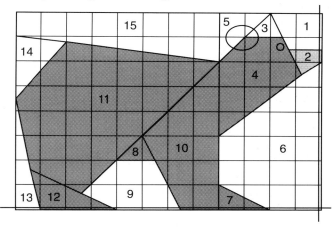

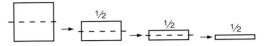
Making Blocks in Odd Sizes

Occasionally, you may wish to make a block in a different size from the standard sizes given. You may need a block that would normally be 9" to be 10" instead. (See the Blue Jay Chain quilt, page 40.) Besides photocopying, there are two ways of making the blocks into odd sizes—drawing a grid or paper folding a grid.

To Draw a Grid:

Draw a square in the size you need for the finished block. Then place your ruler on an angle across the square so that the number of divisions you require (the number of squares in the grid) fits exactly across. For example, to make the Blue Jay (grid of 12 x 12 squares) into a 10" square block, angle the 12" ruler across the square so that the zero point matches with one side of the square, and the 12" mark matches with the other side of the square. Mark a series of dots at the intervals required, which for the Blue Jay would be at the 1" intervals. Draw lines from these dots parallel to the sides of the square. Rotate the square and repeat this procedure across the other two sides. In the example, your 10" square would now have a grid of 12 x 12 squares marked on it.

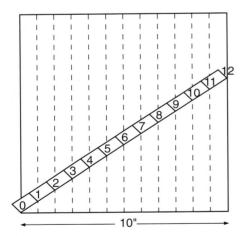

Although some of the blocks are not square, you will start out with a square grid, using the methods above. Make the square the size of the longest side in the block. (For example, to make a Bear block that is 10" on the longest side, use a 10" square.) Once the grid is made, use only the number of squares that the grid requires for the shorter side of the block.

To Paper Fold a Grid:

From a thin sheet of paper, cut out a square the size of the required block. For a block that has a grid of 8 x 8 squares, fold the paper in half to make a rectangle. Fold in half again lengthwise and then fold once more lengthwise (three folds in all). Open out the paper and repeat the three folds in the opposite direction. For a block that has a grid of 12 x 12 squares, fan fold the paper into three equal sections. Fold in half lengthwise and then fold again in half lengthwise (three folds in all). Open out the paper and repeat in the opposite direction.

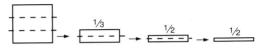

For a grid of 8: fold square in half 3 times.

For a grid of 12: fan fold square into thirds, then in half 2 times.

Using the folded lines on your paper as grid lines, draw the design onto the grid.

Now you are ready to transfer the design to your template material. Two choices are possible here. Use either cardboard, such as tagboard, or template plastic.

Note: This step is already done if you have drawn the design directly onto the plastic template material with a grid.

To Use Cardboard for Templates:

1. Glue the complete photocopy or drawn design onto the cardboard, using a glue stick. Do not use other kinds of paste or glue, which may wet and distort the paper.

   Note: Do not cut out the pieces of the design and then glue to cardboard; always glue the whole design onto cardboard.

2. Cut around the edges of the block, then cut out each piece. Cut longer lines first.

3. Mark grain lines onto the reverse side of each template. It is necessary to mark the grain line on the wrong side of the template because templates are usually used right side down.

   There are two ways to mark the grain line.

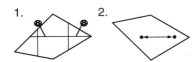

Where one edge is parallel to grain line, flip template over and mark with arrow parallel to edge.

Where there is no edge parallel to grain line:
1. Push pins through template on grain line (grid line);
2. Flip template over to the reverse side and mark the grain line between the two pin holes.

To Use Template Plastic for Templates:

1. Tape or clip the design (either photocopy or drawing) under the plastic. Using marker and ruler, copy the design onto the plastic. Copy the numbers onto each piece and sketch in some kind of pattern to indicate which fabrics are to be used. Copy grain lines onto the templates by copying at least one grid line onto each template piece, marking this line with an arrowhead at each end so that you know it is the grain line. You will be able to see these lines through the plastic when you turn the template upside down to mark.

2. Cut around the edges of the block, then cut out each piece

   To store your templates, keep them in large envelopes—recycled business envelopes are ideal.

Marking and Cutting the Fabric

It is essential to mark all the seam lines for straight-line patchwork. But before marking the fabric, there are two essential points to consider:

1. Which way should the animal face?

Many of the designs in this book are asymmetrical, which just means that the animals either face right or left. To make the design exactly as it is pictured on the page, place the templates, right side down, on the wrong side of the fabric so your pencil lines will be on the wrong side of the fabric. This is the reason why templates must have grain lines marked on their reverse sides.

To make a reverse image of the block (animal facing the opposite way), place the templates right side up on the wrong side of the fabric.

It is important to be clear about this before you begin to mark, so that all your marking is consistent for the block.

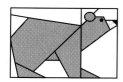

Bear - Mark with templates face down.

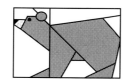

For reverse image, mark with templates face up.

2. Grain line is important.

It is important to keep grain line in mind as you mark your fabrics. The grain of the fabric is the direction in which the threads run on a piece of fabric, both lengthwise and crosswise. The bias grain is at a 45° angle to the lengthwise and crosswise grains. In patchwork it is desirable to have the grain line consistent in a block, wherever this is possible. Sometimes it may not be possible to keep all the

fabrics on grain. For example, you may want to use a patterned fabric, such as stripes, in a particular way. These exceptions are usually not a problem if other pieces in the block are kept on the grain.

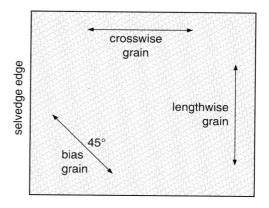

To Mark and Cut the Pieces:

1. Choose your fabrics and then sort all your templates into piles according to the fabrics with which they will be used. Using the bear as an example, make a pile of the pieces that will be black (pieces 4, 7, 8, 9, 10, 11, 12) and a pile for the background (pieces 1, 3, 5, 6, 9, 13, 14, 15). There will be one piece (piece 2) for the muzzle.

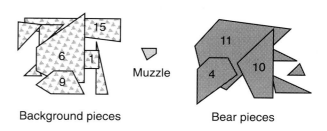

Background pieces   Muzzle   Bear pieces

2. Place fabric on top of the sandpaper board, right side down. Place template on top of fabric, also right side down (or for the reverse image, template right side up). Match the grain of the fabric with the grain line marked on the template.

3. Leave at least ¾" between each piece so that you have enough room to cut a ⅜"-wide seam allowance around each piece. This seam allowance does not have to be measured as you will pin the pieces together along the marked seam line. It is not necessary to mark a cutting line.

   For small pieces and long pointed pieces, leave a generous 1" between pieces so that you can cut a ½"-wide seam allowance. This is very important, since larger seam allowances make it easier to sew small pieces together accurately. The excess seam allowance will be trimmed after the pieces are sewn together.

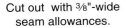

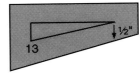

TIP
For small pieces, use big seam allowances!

Cut out with ⅜"-wide seam allowances.

Cut out small and pointed pieces with ½" seam allowances.

4. Using a sharp pencil, mark around the template, making sure that the corners are clearly marked.
5. Write the number of each piece in the seam allowance, so that you can identify pieces after they have been cut out.

Mark with template, right side down, on wrong side of fabric. Write piece number in seam allowance.

6. Mark any "matching marks" that are on the templates onto the fabric. These matching marks are two little crossing lines on some triangles that will help you orient the triangles once they are cut out. Other shapes are not a problem, but with some off-grain triangles, it is easy to get confused about how to lay them out and which edge you should be stitching.

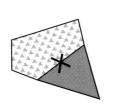
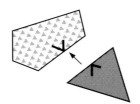

7. Cut out each piece and lay it out in its correct position on your layout board. I find it easiest to lay out each piece as I cut, rather than leaving all the layout until the end.

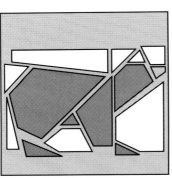

Pinning, Stitching, and Pressing

Just before you sew each seam, pin the pieces together, following this little three-step routine.

1. Push pins through at the corners. Pick up the two pieces to be pinned, keeping them in their correct orientation to each other but placing them right sides together. Push a pin through the right-hand corner of the top piece, then turn the two pieces over and push the pin into the corner of the underneath piece. Repeat the procedure at the other corner.

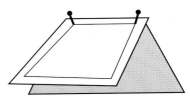

2. Pin at the corners. Holding the fabric pieces at both corners, where the pins are, gently adjust the pieces so marked lines on both sides of the fabric match up. Then anchor both pins by bringing the points up toward the center, not toward the outer edges of the pieces.

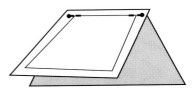

3. Place pins along the length of the line. Pin along the length of the seam, placing pins with their heads pointing to the right. Check both sides to be sure you are pinning along both lines exactly and make any adjustments as needed. Place an extra anchor pin parallel and below the pin at the left-hand corner. This pin will hold the pieces correctly when you take away the first pin as you begin stitching.

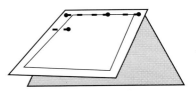

TIP
It is the process of pinning that lines up the fabrics, rather than vice versa. Remember: Pin to line up the fabrics; do not line up the fabrics to pin.

To Machine Piece and Press:

1. Set up your machine with thread suitable for piecing. Generally, white thread is fine, unless all fabrics are dark-colored. Then switch to a dark color. Set stitch length between 10 and 12 stitches per inch to give a neat stitch, but one that is not too difficult to undo should a small correction be necessary.
2. Set up your iron conveniently near your machine.
3. Following the piecing order carefully, pick up the first two pieces to be stitched together and pin as described on page 12. Take out the pin in the left-hand corner and place the cut edge below the needle, lining up the needle with the marked line. Stitch from the cut edge, across the seam allowances, along the marked line, and across the seam allowances at the other side to the cut edges. As you sew, pull out the pins just before they go under the presser foot. Snip the thread ends and trim the seam allowances to an even ¼" after you have stitched the seam.

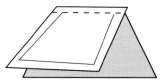

For machine piecing, stitch from cut edge to cut edge along marked line.

4. Press the seams to one side, unless expressly instructed otherwise. (Occasionally, a block will lie flatter if some of the seams are pressed open.) Decide to which side the seam allowances should be pressed, based on the following considerations:
   - Press seams toward the darker fabric so that there is no shadow under the lighter fabric.
   - Press seams in opposite directions at a seam intersection for precisely matched seams that lie flat.
   - Press seams in the direction to which they naturally wish to go. Especially where there are bulky seam intersections, some seam allowances have a mind of their own, so it is best to go with the flow.
   - Press seams away from the lines where quilting will be stitched; it is easier to quilt where there are no bulky seam allowances.
5. When the block is completed, trim the edges of the block so that it is exactly the size required, plus a ¼"-wide seam allowance all around. You can use your rotary cutter and large square ruler to help with this. Be ruthless; ignore any small inaccuracies that may have occurred and trim the block to the precise size required so that it can be conveniently combined with other patchwork blocks.

To Hand Piece and Press:

1. Following the piecing order carefully, pick up and pin pieces together before stitching as described on page 12.
2. Thread your needle with a color to match the darker of the fabrics that you are sewing. Tie a knot at the end of the thread.
3. Begin stitching ⅛" in from one corner of the seam, take a small stitch into the exact corner, then turn and sew along the marked seam line with a running stitch. Pull the pins out as you come to them. When you reach the other corner, sew into it exactly, then turn and take a couple of stitches backward, ending with a backstitch a short distance from the corner. Snip off thread.

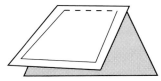

For hand piecing, stitch only along marked line and not into seam allowances.

4. Complete all seams in this manner, following the piecing order. Note that you should not be sewing into any seam allowances (as you would if you were machine piecing); all seam allowances should be left free. When you come to a cross seam, sew right up to it, then push your needle through the seam allowances, leaving them upright, and begin sewing on the other side.
5. When the block is all stitched, trim the seam allowances and press them together to one side, as described for machine piecing.

TIP

In hand piecing, the block is pressed after all seams are completed; with machine piecing, each seam is pressed as you go.

---

6. Trim the edges of the block so that it is exactly the size you need, plus ¼" seam allowance all around.

Cardinal block, 19½" x 19½". Machine quilted.

Robin block, 22" x 22". Machine quilted.

Raccoon block, 23" x 23". Machine quilted.

Hummingbird block, 21¾" x 21¾". Machine quilted.

Blue Jay block, 20" x 20". Machine quilted.

Mallard Duck block 18" x 18". Made and hand quilted by Kathy Burkey.

Squirrel block, 17" x 17". Machine quilted.

PIECING TRADITIONAL BLOCKS and BORDERS

Most of the quilts in this book combine the straight-line patchwork animal blocks with traditional pieced blocks or pieced borders. The traditional blocks can be pieced by hand, or they can be pieced by machine, using modern techniques of speed cutting and machine piecing.

Most traditional blocks are combinations of two simple shapes, the right-angle triangle and the square. Some traditional blocks contain shapes that are made of several of these shapes put together, such as two squares making a rectangle or two triangles making a parallelogram. Underlying all the blocks is a geometric grid of squares, and the key to understanding any block is to work out how many squares can be accurately drawn on top of it. The various combinations of squares have been given names, although the naming system is not entirely logical. A block that breaks down into a grid of 3 x 3 squares is called a nine-patch block, but a block that breaks down into a grid of either 2 x 2 squares or 4 x 4 squares is called a four-patch block. A block that breaks down into a grid of 5 x 5 squares is called a five-patch block, and a grid of 7 x 7 squares is called a seven-patch block. Whatever the names, always remember that most blocks have this underlying structure of squares. Once you know this, you can rapidly work out how to construct any block you want. All of the traditional blocks in this book have a label explaining whether they are four-, five-, seven- or nine-patch blocks.

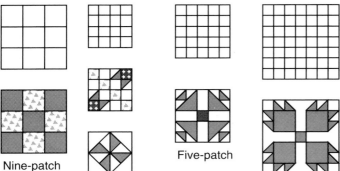

Nine-patch   Four-patch   Five-patch   Seven-patch

The triangles used in traditional blocks are generally created when a square is divided into halves or quarters. Thus, they are conveniently called half-square or quarter-square triangles.

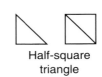
Half-square triangle

Quarter-square triangle

TIP
If you choose to hand piece the blocks, make templates the size you need for the finished piece without adding seam allowances. For example, a 2" square in the finished block would require a 2"-square template. Mark, cut, and stitch the pieces together as described for the straight-line patchwork animal blocks.

Because all the traditional blocks are made up of squares, rectangles, and triangles that are divisions of a square (and not the odd shapes used for straight-line patchwork), it is possible to use "automatic seam allowances." An automatic seam allowance simply means that the width of the seam allowance—¼"—is added to each shape to be sewn, and the piece is cut out exactly to this size. The pieces can then be sewn together by lining up the cut edges and sewing a precise ¼"-wide seam. This technique works with these particular shapes because shapes sit exactly on top of each other, with no guesswork about where the seam will go or how the corners will match up.

A seam allowance of ¼" is ideal because it is a convenient size and because its multiples add up to manageable figures that are generally in quarter, half, or whole inches. But watch triangles—the ¼" must be measured at right angles to the diagonal side so the shapes plus seam allowances will extend by ⅝" at the pointed corners. Quilters' rulers are marked in divisions of ⅛" or ¼", so you can easily add the necessary amounts for seam allowances.

If you use an automatic seam allowance, it is very important that you sew your seams an exact ¼". If you do not, then the different blocks and borders in your quilt will not fit together. Practice making an accurate ¼"-wide seam. A little time spent doing this will save a lot of trouble later on.

> ## TIP
> All cutting instructions for the traditional blocks, patchwork shapes, and borders are given in sizes that include the ¼"-wide seam allowance. The animal blocks and other straight-line patchwork blocks, which are not constructed with automatic seam allowances, are trimmed after the block is completed to make them the finished size required, plus ¼" all around.

Blocks and traditional patchwork shapes can be cut out by using either templates or Template-Free® techniques.

To Use Templates:

1. Make template shapes required for the block from cardboard or template plastic by accurately drawing the finished shape, then adding ¼"-wide seam allowances all around. Be careful with triangles and be sure to make the ¼" at right angles to the diagonal. A Quilter's Quarter can be a great help here.
2. Use templates to mark the fabrics and cut out along the marked lines, which are your cutting lines. Your sandpaper board will be useful for marking.
3. Lay the cutout block on your layout board or square of paper.

To Use Template-Free Methods:

Since there are many excellent books describing these techniques, the procedures will only be briefly described here.

1. Work out the sizes your pieces need to be cut, including the ¼"-wide seam allowance all around. For squares and rectangles, this will be the finished size plus ½". For example, a 4" finished square will be cut 4½" x 4½" (to include the ¼" seam allowances). For triangles, work out what size square to cut so you cut across either one or two diagonals to make triangles the size required. For half-square triangles, cut squares that are ⅞" larger than the shortest sides of the finished triangle.

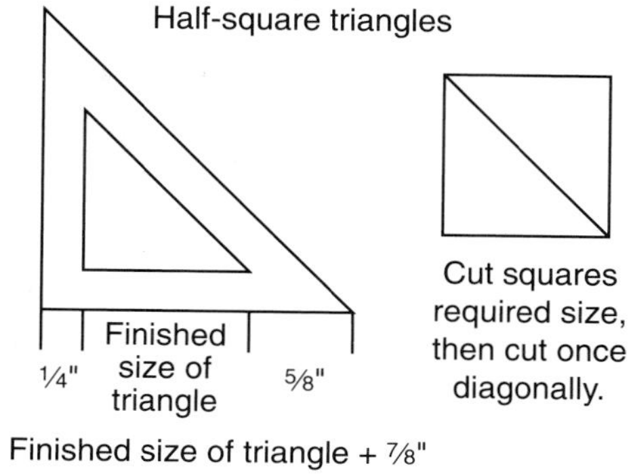

Half-square triangles
Finished size of triangle
¼"
⅝"
Cut squares required size, then cut once diagonally.
Finished size of triangle + ⅞"

For quarter-square triangles, cut squares that are 1¼" larger than the longest side of the finished triangle.

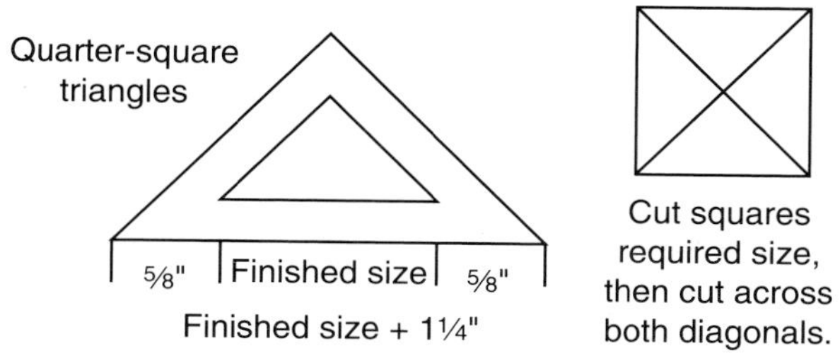

Quarter-square triangles
⅝"
Finished size
⅝"
Finished size + 1¼"
Cut squares required size, then cut across both diagonals.

2. Using your rotary cutter and mat, square up the end of your fabric. Fold fabric in half so that the selvages match and place the fold nearest to you. Put a right triangle or square ruler on the edge of the fold. Position the long ruler up against the right triangle. It should now be at an exact right angle to the fold. Remove the right triangle and cut.

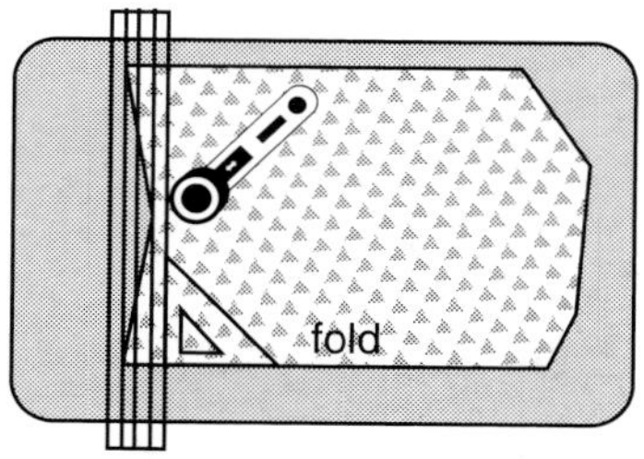

fold

3. Using the long ruler to measure, cut strips the width required. For longer strips and borders, the fabric can be folded again. Generally, strips are cut across the width of the fabric. If longer strips are required, they may be cut along the length of the fabric.

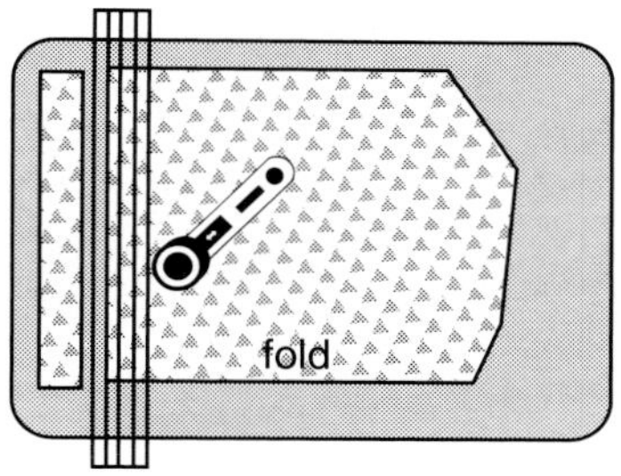

fold

4. For squares and rectangles, crosscut strips into the shapes needed.

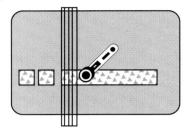

For triangles, first cut the strips into squares, then cut the squares diagonally once or twice as needed.

To make small half-square triangle units quickly and accurately, you can use the Bias Square technique developed by Nancy J. Martin. This technique is especially useful for the Delectable Mountains pattern in the Eagle in the Mountains quilt (page 82). For a full description of the method, see *Back to Square One* by Nancy J. Martin and *Rotary Riot* by Judy Hopkins and Nancy J. Martin. Bias grain refers to the direction of the fabric that is at a 45° angle to the straight grain. (See diagram on page 11.)

To Use the Bias Square Technique:

1. Work out the size of the pieced square you will be cutting. For instance, if you want the finished size of the square to be 2", your cut size will be 2½" to include the ¼" seam allowances.
2. Cut strips of fabric on the bias grain, cutting each strip the same width as the size you determined in step 1. For the example given, your cut size was 2½" square (for finished squares of 2"), so you would cut bias strips 2½" wide.

    If you have a long length of fabric, first cut it into half-yard lengths, then cut the bias strips. Cut strips on the true bias by lining up a right triangle with a straight-grain edge of the fabric. Position your long ruler against the right triangle to create an accurate 45° angle. Remove the right triangle and make the bias cut. Thereafter, cut strips the width required.

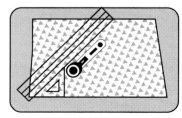

3. Sew the bias strips together, alternating the strips for the two fabrics in each square. Press seams to one side, usually toward the darker fabric.
4. Using the Bias Square® cutting guide, cut squares

from your joined strips by lining up the center line of the Bias Square with the seams you have sewn. Note that some waste triangles will result along the sides of the strips.

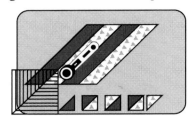

To Sew and Press, Using Automatic Seam Allowances:

1. Set up your machine for sewing an accurate ¼"-wide seam. There are several ways to do this:
    a) If yours is a zigzag machine, move the needle so that it will come down exactly ¼" from the edge of the presser foot. Using a scrap of template plastic (or graph paper) with grid lines spaced ¼" apart, line up the edge of the presser foot with one of the lines, then move the needle so that it will come down exactly on the line that is parallel and ¼" away.
    b) If your machine does not zigzag, mark the ¼" with a strip of masking tape on the bed of the machine. Use a scrap of ¼"-grid template plastic (or graph paper) as a guide for placing the tape.
    c) Purchase a special presser foot for your machine that is exactly ¼" wide from the needle to the side of the foot.
2. Place pieces with right sides together, matching cut edges along the length of the seam. Beginning at the cut edges on one side, sew across the seam allowances along the seam line, which will be exactly ¼" in from the cut edges along the length of the pieces, and finally across the seam allowances to the cut edges at the other side.
3. Press each seam to one side. Follow the same principles for the pressing already described for straight-line patchwork. (See page 13.) Organize your pressing so that seams will be pressed to alternate sides at seam intersections. This will keep seam intersections neat and flat.

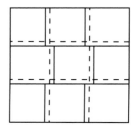

4. While the piecing order is not as specific in traditional patchwork as it is for straight-line patchwork, it is still important to sew the pieces together in the correct order. Generally, small pieces are sewn together into units first, then the units are sewn into rows, and finally the rows are joined to make the block.

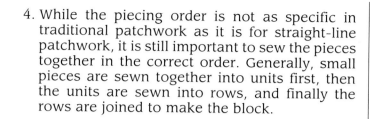

5. Many blocks include triangles that must first be sewn together into squares. If you use the Bias Square method, small triangles are already joined together into squares and are ready to be pieced into the larger block.

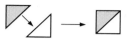

An example is the Road to Oklahoma block.

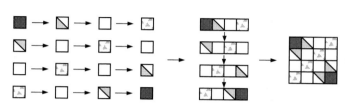

ADDING DETAILS

The addition of details, such as eyes, ears, and legs, make these animals come alive. These details can be added with appliqué and simple embroidery, although another alternative for eyes is to use little black buttons.

Appliqué

While there are many different ways of doing appliqué, the easiest method for the small shapes, such as animal eyes and ears, is by covering a piece of light cardboard in the precise shape you want with fabric.

Circles and Other Small Shapes

1. Cut out the appliqué shape from light cardboard the size of the desired finished shape. Use an appropriately sized button to draw the circle.
2. Cut out the fabric shape ¼" larger than the cardboard shape.

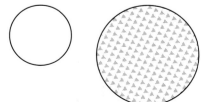

3. Using basting thread in a contrasting color to the fabric, sew a small running stitch about ⅛" in from the edge of the fabric. Begin with a firm knot on the right side of the fabric and end by

bringing the needle out on the right side of the fabric. Leave several inches of the thread end dangling.

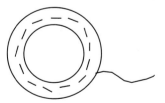

4. Place the cardboard shape in the center of the wrong side of the fabric and pull on both ends of the running stitch so that the fabric gathers closely around the shape. Tie the thread firmly.

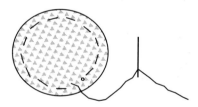

5. Press well, using a steam iron.

6. Remove the running stitch and trim seam allowance to ⅛". Gently remove the cardboard.

7. Baste around the folded edge to hold the seam allowance in place.

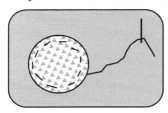

8. Pin prepared shape to the quilt, matching the grain line of the shape to the grain line of the background. Using a thread that matches the prepared shape, appliqué shape in place.

Other Shapes

For larger appliqué shapes, use the method you find most comfortable. I find the following method useful and very accurate.

1. Cut out appliqué shape from light cardboard.
2. Baste or pin paper shape to the wrong side of the fabric, then cut out the fabric, adding ⅛"-wide seam allowances all around.
3. Fold and finger press seam allowances to the back and baste, snipping corners and concave curves as needed.
4. Baste prepared shape to background fabric and appliqué in place.
5. Remove all basting; working from the wrong side, carefully cut away the background fabric behind the appliqué, leaving a ¼"-wide seam allowance. Remove cardboard shape.

Embroidery

You can make eyes, legs, or any other details on the birds and animals with a few simple embroidery stitches.

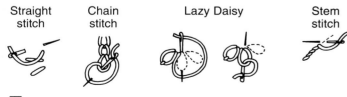

Straight stitch   Chain stitch   Lazy Daisy   Stem stitch

Eyes

An eye can be easily stitched using a chain stitch. Thread your needle with two strands of embroidery thread. First, make a very small, single chain stitch in the center. Then, using a very small chain stitch, embroider a ring of chains around the center stitch. Continue in this manner until the eye is as large as required.

This method of making eyes allows for a color change. You can do the center and the first one or two rows of chain stitch in black, then change to another color around the outside.

When an eye is black on a black background, such as the Canada goose, stitch around the outer edge of the eye with a line of gray stem stitch to make it more visible.

For the eagle, do not embroider a full circle for the eye. Instead, embroider a black center, surround the black with two rows of yellow, then embroider a row of black only around the lower two-thirds of the eye. Give him a brow by stitching a line of black across the top of the eye.

A highlight may be added to the eye by making two small straight stitches in white, at a spot on the eye where you think the light would fall. This may be done to both appliquéd and embroidered eyes. This twinkle will give your animal a realistic look.

Legs

Embroider the legs and feet with a chain stitch or stem stitch, depending on the thickness required. A stem stitch gives a finer line, while a chain stitch gives a thicker one. Make several lines of chain stitching if a heavier line is required. Draw the lines lightly with a pencil first, then embroider over the pencil lines.

Whiskers and Mouths

Embroider other details, such as whiskers on the raccoon and the mouth on the beaver, with a stem stitch, using either one or two strands of embroidery thread. Draw features lightly in pencil, then embroider over the pencil lines.

CONSTRUCTING a QUILT

Assembling the Quilt Top

1. Piece animal block(s), using the straight-line patchwork technique. Piece other blocks as required, such as the Tree block in the Beaver quilt (page 34). Trim blocks to the exact size needed, plus ¼" all around for seam allowances.
2. Piece traditional blocks.
3. Cut fabric for sashing strips and borders.
4. Assemble quilt as shown in the quilt photo for each quilt.

    Generally, sew blocks into rows, then sew rows together to make the center of the quilt top. If sashing is required, sew sashing strips between the blocks to make rows, and then join rows with sashing strips between them.

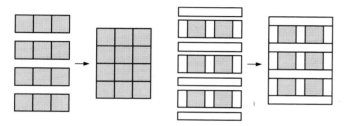

When adding a strip of sashing between two rows of blocks, be careful to line up the blocks exactly opposite each other. Sew the sashing strip to the first row of blocks, then place pins opposite the corners of each block on the other side of the sashing strip. Match the pin marks to the corners of the second row of blocks and stitch together.

Assemble blocks set on point in diagonal rows. Lay out all the blocks, including side and corner triangles, in the correct order before you start sewing. Sew one row at a time, then join rows. Quarter- and half-square triangles are used for the sides and corners of the quilt.

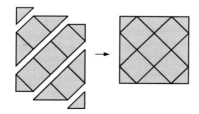

Medallion-style quilts, such as the Canada Goose quilt (page 48) and the Hummingbird quilt (page 52), are made with a block (or blocks) in the center, surrounded by a series of borders. The borders (whether fabric strips or pieced strips) are added, working from the center outward.

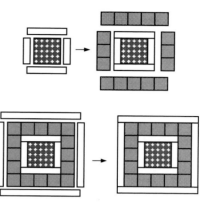

5. Add borders with straight-cut or mitered corners.

For Straight-Cut Corners:

Measure the length of the quilt top at the center from raw edge to raw edge. Cut two borders to that measurement. Mark the centers of the border strips and the sides of the quilt top. Join border strips to the sides of the quilt, matching ends and centers and easing as necessary.

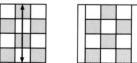

Measure the width of the quilt top at the center from raw edge to raw edge, including the border pieces you just added. Cut two border strips to that measurement. Mark the centers of the border strips and the top and bottom of the quilt top. Join border strips to the top and bottom of the quilt, matching ends and centers and easing as necessary.

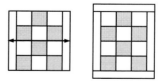

For Mitered Corners:

Estimate the finished outside dimensions of your quilt, including borders. Cut four border strips to this length, plus 2"-3" extra. If your quilt is to have multiple borders, sew the individual strips together and treat the resulting unit as a single piece for mitering. In this case, the excess strip length must be greater than the combined width of the seamed strips.

Mark ¼" seam intersections on all four corners of quilt top and centers of each side.

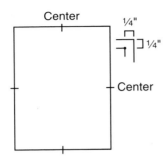

Mark the centers of border strips as well as each end where the corners of the quilt will be.

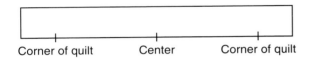

Sew the strips in place so the stitching does not extend into the ¼"-wide seam allowance on either side of the corner. Center each border strip, matching the center pins and the pins in the border strip to the corners of the quilt top. Stitch from mark to mark.

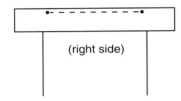

The stitching lines must meet exactly at the corners but must not overlap.

Complete each of the corners, using the following procedure: Fold the quilt diagonally so that the strips at each corner are aligned, with right sides together. Using a right triangle or quilters' ruler marked with a 45° angle, draw a line from the corner where the border strips meet to the outside edge of the border.

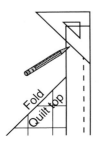

Secure border with pins and stitch on the pencil line. Check the accuracy and flatness of the seam before trimming seam allowances. Press seams open.

Quilting

Quilting may be done by hand or machine. Patterns for quilting are many and varied. You can outline the patchwork pieces; you can fill in spaces with grids and/or specific designs; or you can do free-form quilting across the quilt surface. Mark quilting designs before or after the layers are put together.

To Mark Before the Layers Are Put Together:

Use a sharp #2 pencil and mark lightly. Long rulers are helpful in drawing straight-line grids. Cut quilting-pattern templates or stencils from plastic or cardboard; then draw around them on the quilt top. Or trace quilting patterns onto the quilt top by placing it on a light box or by taping both the pattern and quilt top to a window.

To Mark After the Layers Are Put Together:

Use chalk or masking tape to mark quilting designs just prior to stitching. Do not leave masking tape on the quilt top any longer than necessary, to avoid marks from the tape.

Hand Quilting

1. Prepare backing, piecing as necessary. Cut it 2" larger than the quilt top all around. Cut batting the same size as the backing.
2. Press quilt top and mark quilting designs.
3. Layer the backing, batting, and quilt top, making sure all layers are smooth and wrinkle-free.
4. Pin and baste the layers together, making a grid of basting stitches about 4" to 6" apart. Always pin or baste from the center of the quilt out toward the edges.
5. Place the quilt in a hoop or frame, making sure that the layers are smooth and free of wrinkles.
6. Use a quilting thread and a between needle in a size that you find comfortable. Quilt layers together, using a small, even running stitch. The needle goes down vertically until touched by your finger beneath the quilt. It is then rocked back upward to make a small stitch. This action is repeated for several stitches before the thread is pulled through. Use thimbles to protect your fingers. Begin quilting with a knot that can be gently pulled into the batting and end with a little backstitch, then run the thread through into the batting and snip off. If you are using chalk or masking tape, mark only the small section you are about to stitch; complete this

section before marking the next section.

7. Remove the basting when quilting is completed.

Machine Quilting

Machine quilting is especially suited to small projects. The major limitation of machine quilting a large quilt is managing the bulk of the quilt under the arm of the sewing machine. This limitation can be overcome either by quilting an allover straight-line grid pattern (where the quilt is tightly rolled up and moved through the machine like a long sausage) or by making the quilt in smaller sections that can be joined together later. Seams on the back can be covered with appliquéd strips of fabric.

I recommend safety pinning the quilt layers together for machine quilting, since pinning holds the layers more firmly than basting.

1. Cut backing (piecing as necessary) 2" larger than the quilt top. Firm, 100% cotton fabrics are especially suitable here.
2. Choose a thin, firm batting for machine quilting. Cut the batting the same size as the backing.
3. Press quilt top and mark any quilting designs.
4. Layer backing, batting, and quilt top, making sure all layers are smooth. Working from the center outward, pin the layers together with safety pins, but do not close the pins at this stage. When you have checked to see that there are no wrinkles on the back, close the safety pins. If you close the pins when you first put them in, the action of closing the pin may lift and rumple the layers.
5. Set up your sewing machine with plenty of clear table space beside and behind it. Attach a walking foot to the machine if you have one. This foot helps the three layers move smoothly together through the machine. Choose quilting thread to match or contrast with the quilt top, or use a clear, monofilament thread that will blend into all colors. This thread also comes in a dark shade for dark fabrics. Fill bobbin with a thread to match the backing fabric. Do not use monofilament thread on the bobbin.
6. If the quilt is large, it will have to be rolled or folded neatly to fit under the machine.
7. Machine stitch the quilting design as desired. Make sure that all three layers go through the machine evenly, using your fingers and hands to smooth the layers sideways in front of the presser foot. If you are using chalk or masking tape, mark only the small section you are about to sew; complete this section before marking the next section.
8. Remove safety pins.

Binding

Finish the quilt with a binding around the outside edge. I prefer to use a double binding.

1. Cut strips the width required, which is four times the finished width plus ½" for seam allowances. For example, cutting strips 2½" wide makes a ½"-wide finished binding.
2. Measure the length and width of the quilt at the centers from raw edge to raw edge. Cut binding strips to required lengths, piecing as necessary. Fold strips in half lengthwise, wrong sides together, and press.
3. Sew binding to the sides of the quilt first. Finger press binding away from the center of the quilt.

4. Sew binding to the top and bottom of the quilt.

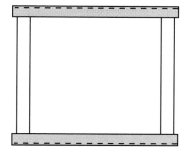

5. Fold binding over to the back of the quilt and blindstitch in place. Corners can be straight cut or mitered.

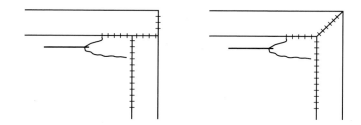

BLACK BEAR BLOCK

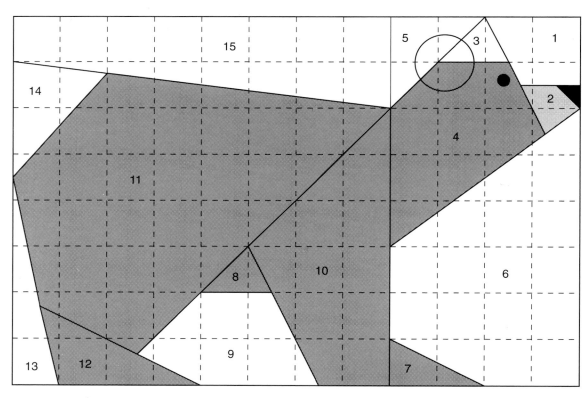

Block size shown: 4" x 6"   1 square = ½"

Color photos on pages 26 and 29.

Size Options

To enlarge from the grid (8 x 12 squares):
    For 6" x 9" block, each square = ¾"
    For 8" x 12" block, each square = 1"
To enlarge by photocopying:
    For 6" x 9" block, enlarge by 150%.
    For 8" x 12" block, enlarge by 200% in 2 steps:
        1. 150%
        2. 133%

Follow this color key if you wish to make the black bear in its natural coloration.

☐ Muzzle (brown) - 2
▨ Body (black) - 4, 7, 8, 10, 11, 12
☐ Background - 1, 3, 5, 6, 9, 13, 14, 15

Piecing Order

A. 1 + 2
B. 3 + 4
C. (1-2) + (3-4) + 5
D. (1-5) + 6 + 7

~~~~~~

E. 8 + 9
F. (8-9) + 10
G. (8-10) + 11
H. (8-11) + 12
I. (8-12) + 13 + 14
J. (8-14) + 15

~~~~~~

K. (1-7) + (8-15)
L. Appliqué ear; embroider nose and eye.

Black Bear Piecing Order

It's as easy as 1, 2, 3, if you just follow the steps in the piecing order.

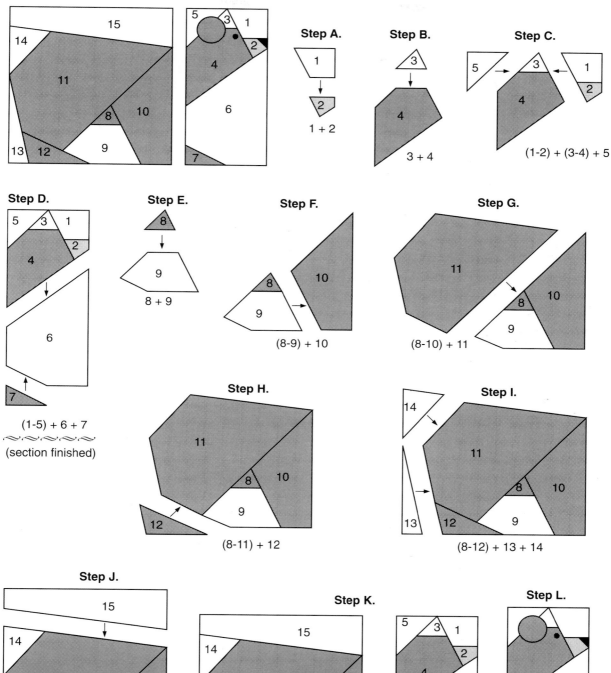

Step A.
1 → 2
1 + 2

Step B.
3 → 4
3 + 4

Step C.
5 → 3 ← 1, 2, 4
(1-2) + (3-4) + 5

Step D.
(1-5) + 6 + 7
(section finished)

Step E.
8 → 9
8 + 9

Step F.
(8-9) + 10

Step G.
(8-10) + 11

Step H.
(8-11) + 12

Step I.
(8-12) + 13 + 14

Step J.
(8-14) + 15
(section finished)

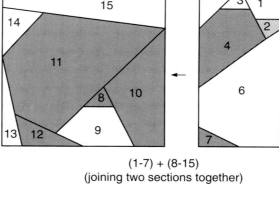

Step K.
(1-7) + (8-15)
(joining two sections together)

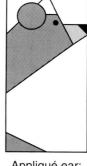

Step L.
Appliqué ear; embroider nose and eye.

BEAR'S PAW QUILT

Bear's Paw quilt, 49½" x 49½". Bears decorate the border of this quilt, which uses the classic favorite pattern, the Bear's Paw. Machine quilted.

Bear Block
Finished Size: 6" x 9"
Enlarge block on page 24 by 150% or use a grid with ¾" squares.

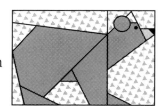

Bear's Paw Block
Finished Size: 10½" x 10½"
Seven-patch block
1 square = 1½"

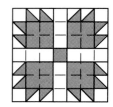

Materials: 44"-wide fabric

1⅓ yds. beige-and-blue print for outer border, background of Bear blocks, and binding
1 yd. beige print for background of Bear's Paw blocks and sashing
¼ yd. dark red print for inner border
⅛ yd. each of 9 assorted blue and dark red prints for Bear's Paw blocks
4 small pieces of assorted navy prints for bears
1 small piece of maroon print for bears' muzzles
54" x 54" piece of batting
3 yds. backing fabric
Embroidery floss in black, tan, and white

Directions

Bear Blocks

1. Cut and piece 4 Bear blocks, using the straight-line patchwork technique on pages 6–13. Make 1 bear a reverse image by using the templates face up when you mark them onto the fabric. Make each bear from a different navy print, with a maroon print muzzle.
2. Appliqué navy print circles (to match bear) for bear's ear (page 19). Embroider tan eyes with a black center and add a white highlight (page 20).
3. Trim each block to 6½" x 9½".

Bear's Paw Blocks

1. From the beige background print, cut:
   36 squares, each 2" x 2"
   36 rectangles, each 2" x 5"
   72 squares, each 2⅜" x 2⅜"; cut once diagonally to yield 144 half-square triangles
2. From each of the 9 prints, cut:
   1 square, each 2" x 2" (9 total)
   4 squares, each 3½" x 3½" (36 total)
   8 squares, each 2⅜" x 2⅜"; cut once diagonally to yield 16 half-square triangles (144 total)
3. Sew background and print half-square triangles together to make 144 pieced squares.
4. Piece 9 Bear's Paw blocks, following the piecing diagram below.

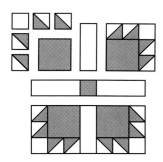

Quilt Top Assembly

1. From the beige print, cut 6 sashing strips, each 2" x 11", and 2 strips, each 2" x 35".
2. Assemble Bear's Paw blocks into 3 rows of 3 blocks each, using the short sashing strips between the blocks.

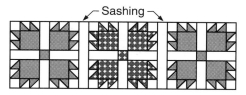

← Sashing →

3. Join the rows of blocks together, using the long sashing strips between each row.

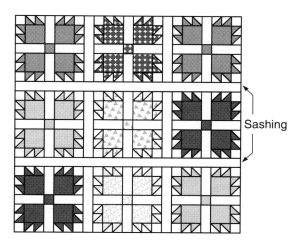

Sashing

4. From the dark red print, cut 4 inner border strips, each 2" wide, cutting across the fabric width. Measure the quilt through the center for the correct side border length as shown on page 21. Trim 2 inner border strips to this length and sew to opposite sides of the quilt top. Repeat measuring and trimming with the remaining strips and sew to the top and bottom edges of the quilt top.

5. From the beige-and-blue print, cut 4 outer border strips, each 6½" wide, cutting across the fabric width.
6. Join a Bear block to the left end of each of 2 of the outer border strips. Set the other 2 strips aside.

Make 2.

Measure the quilt for the outer side borders. Trim the 2 border strips with bears to the correct length and sew to opposite sides of the quilt top.

7. Cut a 6½" x 6½" square and a 3½" x 6½" rectangle from the outer border fabric. Sew a Bear block to 1 of the remaining outer border strips, adding the 6½" square as shown.

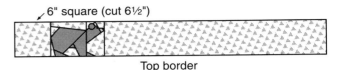

6" square (cut 6½")

Top border

Sew the reverse Bear block to the last remaining outer border strip, adding the 3½" x 6½" rectangle as shown.

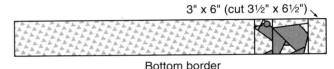

3" x 6" (cut 3½" x 6½")

Bottom border

8. Measure the quilt top for the correct border length and trim the top and bottom borders to this length. Sew to the top and bottom edges of the quilt top.

Quilt Finishing

1. Layer the quilt top with batting and backing; baste.
2. Quilt in the design of your choice.
3. Bind the quilt with 3"-wide, straight-grain strips cut from the beige-and-blue print. You will need approximately 205" of binding.

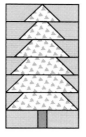

HONEY BEAR QUILT

Honey Bear quilt, 18½" x 21". A black bear hunts for honey in a tree, chased by a swarm of embroidered bees. Machine quilted.

Bear Block
Finished Size: 6" x 9"
Enlarge block on page 24 by 150%, or use a grid with ¾" squares.

Tree Block
Finished Size: 10½" x 6"
7 x 4 squares
1 square = 1½"

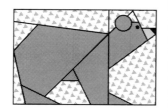

Materials: 44"-wide fabric
¼ yd. black print for outer border and binding
¼ yd. light green print for background
¼ yd. dark green print for Tree block and inner border
Small piece of solid black for bear
1 scrap of light brown print for bear's muzzle
1 scrap of dark brown print for tree trunk
23" x 25" piece of batting
¾ yd. backing fabric
Embroidery floss in black, tan, yellow, and white

Tree Block

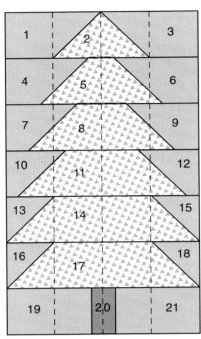

Block size shown: 2" x 3½"
1 square = ½"

To enlarge from the grid:
   For 10½" x 6" block, each square = 1½"
To enlarge by photocopying:
   For 10½" x 6" block, enlarge by 300% in 3 steps.
      1. 150%
      2. 150%
      3. 133%

Piecing Order
   A.   1 + 2 + 3
   B.   4 + 5 + 6
   C.   7 + 8 + 9
   D.   10 + 11 + 12
   E.   13 + 14 + 15
   F.   16 + 17 + 18
   G.   19 + 20 + 21
   H.   (1-3) + (4-6) + (7-9) + (10-12) + (13-15) +
        (16-18) + (19-21)

Directions

Bear Block
1. Cut and piece the Bear block, using the straight-line patchwork technique on pages 6–13. Make bear from black solid, with light brown print muzzle.
2. Appliqué black circle for bear's ear (page 19). Embroider tan eyes with a black center and add a white highlight (page 20).
3. Trim block to 6½" x 9½".

Tree Block
1. Cut and piece Tree block, using the straight-line patchwork technique.
2. Trim Tree block to 11" x 6½"

Quilt Top Assembly
1. From the background print, cut a rectangle 7" x 9½". Sew above Bear block.
2. From the background print, cut a rectangle 2½" x 6½". Sew above Tree block.
3. Join Bear block and Tree block together.
4. Embroider bees above bear as shown in photo on page 29. Using 2 strands of black embroidery floss, embroider bee head and body with chain stitch: Make 2 vertical chain stitches, one inside the other, for the head; make 2 horizontal chain stitches, one inside the other, for the thorax; and make 3 longer chain stitches, one inside the other, for the abdomen. Add straight stitches for legs. Using a single strand of white embroidery floss, make a large chain for the wing, tacking the chain down in 2 places to round the wing shape and adding a single straight stitch down the center to make a vein. Using 2 strands of yellow embroidery floss, make 3 stripes across the abdomen with straight stitches.

Bee

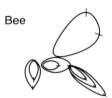

5. From the dark green print, cut 2 inner border strips, each 1½"-wide, cutting across the fabric width. From 1 strip, cut 2 pieces, each 13" long, and sew to opposite sides of the quilt top. From remaining strip, cut 2 pieces, each 17½" long, and sew to the top and bottom edges of the quilt top.
6. From the black print, cut 2 outer border strips, each 2½" wide, cutting across the fabric width. Cut both strips into 2 pieces, one 15" long and the other 21½" long. Sew the 15" strips to the sides of the quilt top and the 21½" strips to the top and bottom.

Quilt Finishing
1. Layer the quilt top with batting and backing; baste.
2. Quilt in the design of your choice.
3. Bind the quilt with 2½"-wide, straight-grain strips cut from the black print. You will need approximately 80" of binding.

BEAVER BLOCK

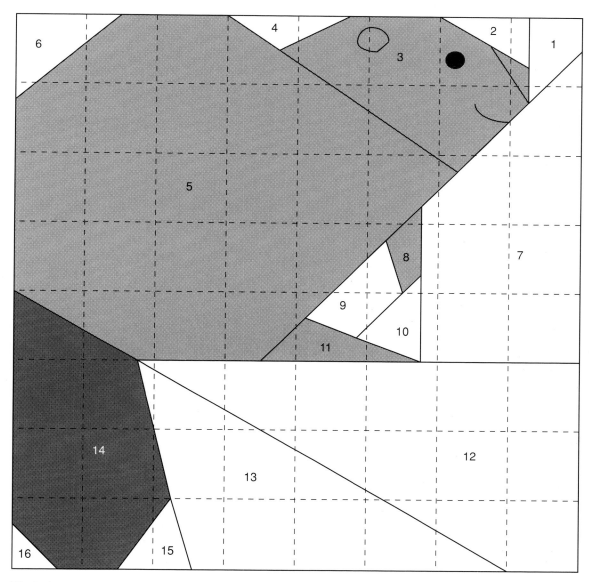

Block size shown: 6" x 6"   1 square = ¾"

Color photos on pages 33 and 35.

Size Options

To enlarge from the grid (8 x 8 squares):
    For 8" x 8" block, each square = 1"
    For 10" x 10" block, each square = 1¼"
    For 12" x 12" block, each square = 1½"
To enlarge by photocopying:
    For 8" x 8" block, enlarge by 133%.
    For 10" x 10" block, enlarge by 167% in 2 steps:
        1. 150%
        2. 111%
    For 12" x 12" block, enlarge by 200% in 2 steps:
        1. 150%
        2. 133%

Follow this color key if you wish to make the beaver in its natural coloration.

■ Beaver body (brown) - 3, 5, 8, 11

■ Tail (dark brown) - 14

□ Background - 1, 2, 4, 6, 7, 9, 10, 12, 13, 15, 16

Piecing Order

A. 2 + 3 + 4
B. 1 + (2-4)
C. 5 + 6
D. (1-4) + (5-6)

~~~~~~

E. 8 + 9
F. (8-9) + 10
G. (8-10) + 11
H. 7 + (8-11)

~~~~~~

I. (1-6) + (7-11)
J. (1-11) + 12

~~~~~~

K. 14 + 15 + 16
L. 13 + (14-16)

~~~~~~

M. (1-12) + (13-16)
N. Embroider eye and mouth; appliqué or embroider nose and ear.

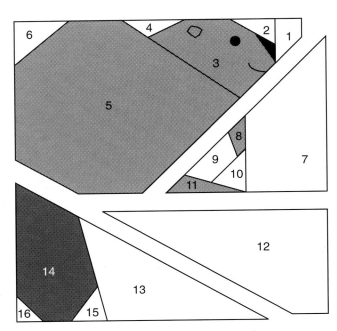

Major block sections

BEAVER QUILT

Beaver quilt, 32" x 32". Simple trees make an appropriate border around a beaver. Machine quilted.

Beaver Block
Finished Size: 12" x 12"
Enlarge block on page 31
by 200% or use a grid with
1½" squares.

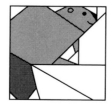

Tree Block
Finished Size: 5" x 5"
1 square = 1"

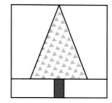

Materials: 44"-wide fabric
¾ yd. beige print for background
½ yd. green plaid for border
¼ yd. brown print for beaver and tree trunks
Assorted green print scraps at least 4" x 4" for trees
    and corner squares
Scrap of dark brown print or solid for tail, nose,
    and ear
Small black button for eye
¼ yd. red print or solid for binding
36" x 36" piece of batting
1 yd. backing fabric
Embroidery floss in dark brown

Tree Block

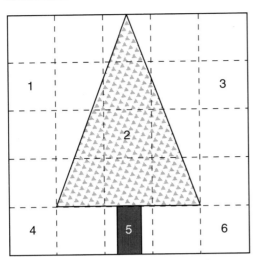

Block size shown: 2½" x 2½"
1 square = ½"

To enlarge from the grid (5 x 5 squares):
  For 5" x 5" block, each square = 1"
To enlarge by photocopying:
  For 5" x 5" block, enlarge by 200% in 2 steps:
    1. 150%
    2. 133%

Piecing Order
A. 1 + 2 + 3
B. 4 + 5 + 6
C. (1-3) + (4-6)

Directions

Beaver Block
1. Cut and piece the Beaver block, using the straight-line patchwork technique on pages 6–13. Cut the beaver body from the brown print and the tail from the dark brown print.
2. Sew on black button for eye; embroider mouth, using brown embroidery floss (page 20). Appliqué dark brown nose and ear (page 19).
3. Trim block to 12½" x 12½".
4. From the background print, cut 2 sashing strips, each 2" x 12½" and sew to the sides of the Beaver block. Cut 2 sashing strips, each 2" x 15½". Sew to the top and bottom edge of the Beaver block.

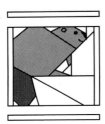

Tree Blocks
1. Cut and piece 16 Tree blocks, using the straight-line patchwork technique on pages 6–13.
2. Trim each block to 5½" x 5½".

Quilt Top Assembly
1. Arrange the Tree blocks around the Beaver block, creating a pleasing balance of color and print.
2. Sew the Tree blocks together in vertical strips of 3 for each side of the block, and horizontal strips of 5 for the top and bottom of the block. Stitch tree strips to the sides and then to the top and bottom of the block.

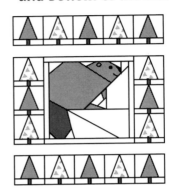

3. From green plaid, cut 4 strips, each 4" wide, cutting across the fabric width. From green prints, cut 4 squares, each 4" x 4".
4. Measure the quilt across the center for the correct border length as shown on page 21. Trim the 4"-wide strips to this length. Stitch to opposite sides of the quilt top. Press seams toward the borders.
5. Sew a 4" green square to each short end of the 2 remaining border strips.
6. Sew borders with corner squares to the top and bottom edges of the quilt top.

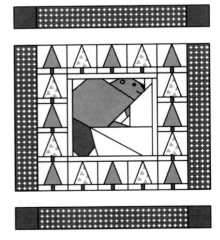

Quilt Finishing
1. Layer the quilt top with batting and backing; baste.
2. Quilt in the design of your choice.
3. Bind the quilt with 2½"-wide, straight-grain strips cut from the red fabric. You will need approximately 132" of binding.

EAGER BEAVER QUILT

Eager Beaver quilt, 51" x 41". A happy beaver contemplates his handiwork amongst the trees. Machine quilted.

Beaver Block
Finished Size: 8" x 8"
Enlarge block on page 31 by 133% or use a grid with 1" squares.

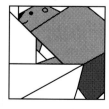

Tree Block
Finished Size: 10" x 10"
Enlarge block on page 36 by 333% in 3 steps:
1. 150%
2. 150%
3. 149%
OR use a grid with 2½" squares.

Materials: 44"-wide fabric
1¼ yds. light brown print for background
1 yd. green print for outer border and binding
¼ yd. each of 6 assorted green prints for trees
¼ yd. red print for inner border
Small piece of brown print for beaver
Small piece of dark brown print for beaver tail
Scraps of brown prints for tree trunks
55" x 45" piece of batting
1¼ yds. backing fabric
Embroidery floss in black and white

Tree Block

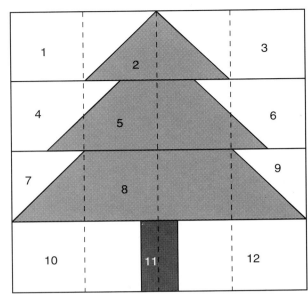

Block size shown: 3" x 3"
1 square = ¾"

Piecing Order
A. 1 + 2 + 3
B. 4 + 5 + 6
C. 7 + 8 + 9
D. 10 + 11 + 12
E. (1-3) + (4-6) + (7-9) + (10-12)

Half Tree Block

Finished Size: 10" x 5"
Enlarge block by 333% in 3 steps:
    1. 150%   2. 150%   3. 149%
OR use a grid with 2½" squares.
(Adapt templates and piecing order from Tree block.)

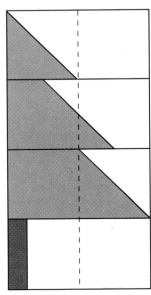

Block size shown: 3" x 1½"
1 square = ¾"

Fallen Tree Block

Finished Size: 10" x 10"
Enlarge block by 333% in 3 steps:
    1. 150%
    2. 150%
    3. 149%
OR use a grid with 2½" squares.

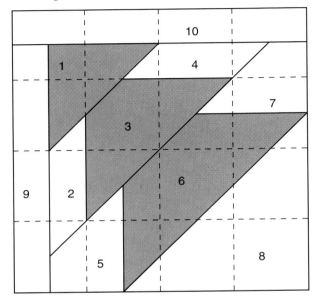

Block size shown: 3" x 3"
1 square = ¾"

Piecing Order
A. 2 + 3 + 4
B. 5 + 6 + 7
C. 1 + (2-4) + (5-7) + 8
D. (1-8) + 9
E. (1-9) + 10

Stump Block

Finished Size: 10" x 5"
Enlarge block by 333%
in 3 steps:
    1. 150%
    2. 150%
    3. 149%
OR use a grid with
2½" squares.

Piecing Order
A. 1 + 2 + 3
B. (1-3) + 4
C. (1-4) + 5
D. (1-5) + 6

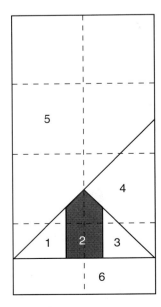

Block size shown: 3" x 1½"
1 square = ¾"

Directions

Beaver Block

1. Cut and piece 1 Beaver block, using the straight-line patchwork technique on pages 6–13. Be sure to make the beaver a reverse image by placing the templates face up when you mark them onto the fabric.
2. Embroider black eyes and add a white highlight (page 20). Outline embroider mouth, nose, and ear with black.
3. Trim block to 8½" x 8½".
4. From the background print, cut 2 sashing strips, each 1½" x 8½" and sew to the sides of the Beaver block. Cut 2 sashing strips, each 1½" x 10½", and sew to the top and bottom edges of the Beaver block.

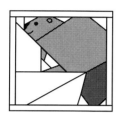

Tree Blocks

1. Cut and piece 8 Tree blocks, 3 Half Tree blocks, 1 Fallen Tree block, and 1 Stump block, using the straight-line patchwork technique on pages 6–13.
2. Trim full Tree blocks to 10½" x 10½" and Half Tree blocks to 10½" x 5½".

Quilt Top Assembly

1. Arrange the blocks into rows as shown below, creating a pleasing balance of color and print. Sew the blocks into rows, then sew rows together to make the center section of the quilt.

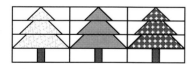

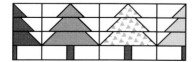

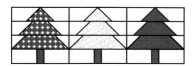

2. From the red print, cut 4 inner border strips, each 1¼" wide. Measure the quilt through the center for the correct side border length as shown on page 21. Trim 2 inner border strips to this length and sew to opposite sides of the quilt top. Repeat measuring and trimming with the remaining strips and sew to the top and bottom edges of the quilt top.
3. From the green print, cut 4 outer border strips, each 5¼" wide, cutting across the fabric width. Measure the quilt through the center for the correct side border length. Trim 2 outer border strips to this length and sew to opposite sides of the quilt top. Repeat measuring and trimming with the remaining strips and sew to the top and bottom edges of the quilt top.

Quilt Finishing

1. Layer the quilt top with batting and backing; baste.
2. Quilt in the design of your choice.
3. Bind the quilt with 2½"-wide, straight-grain strips cut from the green print. You will need approximately 184" of binding.

BLUE JAY BLOCK

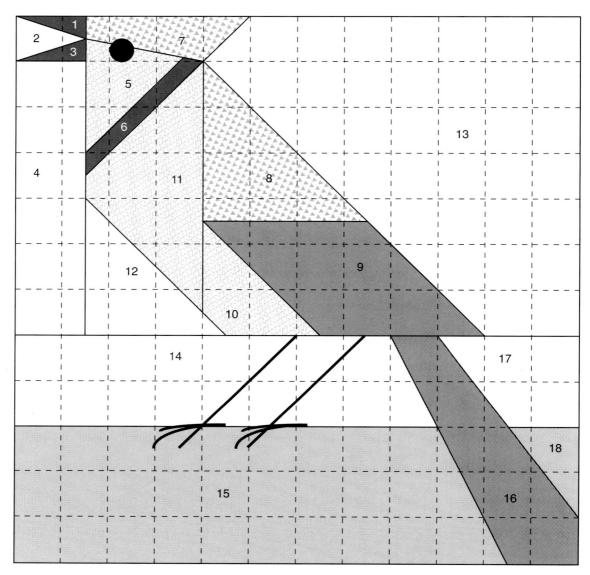

Block size shown: 6" x 6"   1 square = ½"

Color photos on pages 15 and 40.

Size Options

To enlarge from the grid (12 x 12 squares):
    For 9" x 9" block, each square = ¾"
    For 10" x 10" block, see "Making Blocks in Odd
        Sizes" on page 10.
    For 12" x 12" block, each square = 1"
To enlarge by photocopying:
    For 9" x 9" block, enlarge by 150%.
    For 10" x 10" block, enlarge by 167% in 2 steps:
        1. 150%
        2. 111%
For 12" x 12" block, enlarge by 200% in 2 steps:
    1. 150%
    2. 133%

Follow this color key if you wish to make the blue jay in its natural coloration.

- Beak and necklace (black) - 1, 3, 6
- Crest and upper wing (blue) - 7, 8
- Lower wing and tail (dark blue) - 9, 16
- Neck and breast (white or pale gray) - 5, 10, 11
- Fence - 15, 18
- Background - 2, 4, 12, 13, 14, 17

Piecing Order

A. 1 + 2 + 3 + 4

B. 5 + 6
C. (5-6) + 7

D. 8 + 9
E. (8-9) + 10
F. (8-10) + 11
G. (8-11) + 12 + 13

H. (5-7) + (8-13)
I. (1-4) + (5-13)

J. 14 + 15
K. 17 + 18
L. (14-15) + 16 + (17-18)

M. (1-13) + (14-18)
N. Appliqué eye; embroider legs.

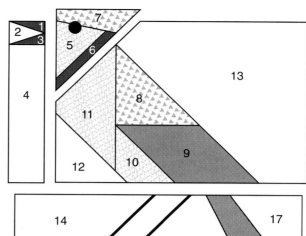

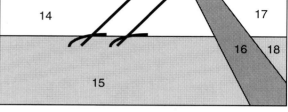

Major block sections

BLUE JAY CHAIN QUILT

Blue Jay Chain quilt, 86" x 62". A classic favorite, the Chain patchwork design is given a new twist with blue jays in the alternate blocks. Machine quilted by Lee Cleland.

Blue Jay Block
Finished Size: 10" x 10"
Enlarge block on page 38 by 167%.

Chain Block
Finished Size: 10" x 10"
Five-patch block
1 square = 2"

Partial Chain Block
Finished Size: 6" x 10"
1 square = 2

Materials: 44"-wide fabric

2¾ yds. white print for background of Bird blocks, Chain blocks, sashing, and pieced inner border
2¼ yds. blue print for outer border and binding
1⅓ yds. total of assorted blue prints to make birds, fences, and blue squares in Chain blocks (Include dark prints for the birds' lower wings and tails and light prints for the fences.)
¼ yd. pale blue print for breasts of birds
⅛ yd. black print for beaks and necklaces of birds
Small piece of black solid for birds' eyes
90" x 66" piece of batting
5 yds. backing fabric
Embroidery floss in black and white

Directions

Blue Jay Blocks

1. Cut and piece 7 Blue Jay blocks, using the straight-line patchwork technique on pages 6–13. Use a variety of blue prints, making the head and upper wing medium blue, lower wing and tail dark blue, and the fence light blue. For all birds, use the same black print for beaks and necklaces, and the same pale blue print for breasts.
2. Appliqué black circles for eyes (page 19). Embroider legs and feet with black floss and embroider white highlight on each eye (page 20).
3. Trim each block to 10½" x 10½".

Chain Blocks

1. From the background fabric, cut:
   50 squares, each 2½" x 2½"
   30 rectangles, each 2½" x 6½"
   12 rectangles each 2½" x 4½"
2. From assorted blue prints, cut 126 squares, each 2½" x 2½". Set aside 24 of these for the sashing.
3. Piece 8 Chain blocks as shown.

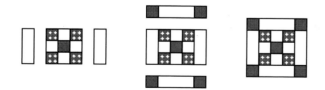

4. Piece 6 partial Chain blocks as shown.

Quilt Top Assembly

1. From background print, cut 38 sashing strips, each 2½" x 10½".
2. Assemble 6 horizontal sashing strips, alternating blue sashing squares with white sashing strips. Each strip should begin and end with a sashing square.
3. Use remaining white sashing strips to join completed Blue Jay blocks in rows of 3 as shown.

Make 3 rows.

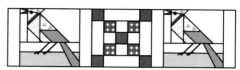

Make 2 rows.

4. Join rows of blocks with sashing strips, following the quilt photo on page 40.
5. From background fabric, cut:
   6 rectangles, each 6½" x 14½"
   4 rectangles, each 6½" x 20½"
6. Assemble the 14½" rectangles with the partial Chain blocks to make 2 strips. Sew to the sides of the quilt.

7. Assemble the 20½" strips to remaining partial Chain blocks and stitch to top and bottom of quilt top.

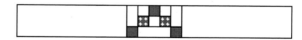

8. From the blue print for outer border, cut 4 strips, each 6½" wide, from the length of the fabric. Measure the quilt through the center for the correct side border length as shown on page 21. Trim 2 border strips to this length and sew to opposite sides of the quilt top. Repeat measuring and trimming with the remaining strips and sew to the top and bottom edges of the quilt top.

Quilt Finishing

1. Layer the quilt top with batting and backing; baste.
2. Quilt in the design of your choice.
3. Bind the quilt with 3"-wide, straight-grain strips cut from the blue outer border print. You will need approximately 296" of binding.

CARDINAL BLOCK

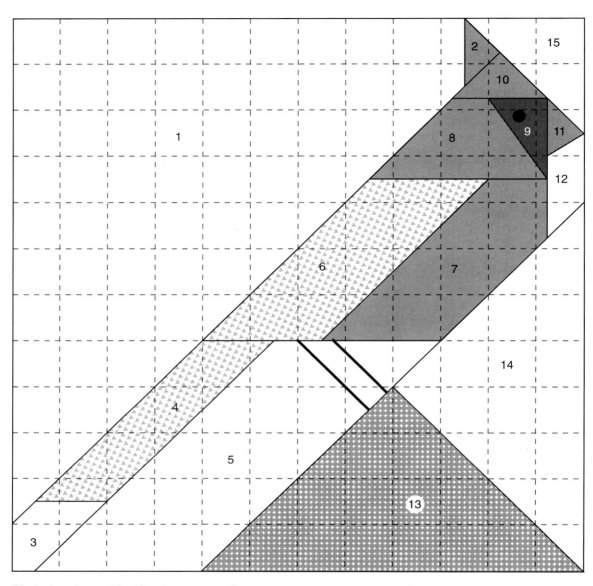

Block size shown: 6" x 6"   1 square = ½"

Color photos on pages 14 and 44.

Size Options

To enlarge from the grid (12 x 12 squares):
    For 9" x 9" block, each square = ¾"
    For 12" x 12" block, each square = 1"
To enlarge by photocopying:
    For 9" x 9" block, enlarge by 150%.
    For 12" x 12" block, enlarge by 200% in 2 steps:
        1. 150%
        2. 133%

Follow this color key if you wish to make the cardinal in its natural coloration.

Head, beak, upper body, and breast (red) - 2, 7, 8, 10, 11

Eye patch (black) - 9

Wing and tail (dark red) - 4, 6

Perch - 13

Background - 1, 3, 5, 12, 14, 15

Alternative color for 9" block - Combine pieces 6, 7, and 8 into 1 piece, and use 1 red fabric for all of the bird.

Piecing Order

A. 1 + 2

≈≈≈≈≈≈

B. 3 + 4
C. (3-4) + 5
D. 6 + 7
E. 8 + 9
F. (3-5) + (6-7) + (8-9) + 10
G. 11 + 12
H. (3-10) + (11-12)

≈≈≈≈≈≈

I. 13 + 14

≈≈≈≈≈≈

J. (1-2) + (3-12) + (13-14)

≈≈≈≈≈≈

K. (1-14) + 15
L. Embroider eye and legs.

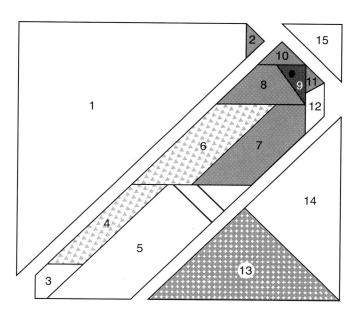

Major block sections

CARDINAL QUILT

Cardinal quilt, 40" x 40". The Cardinal blocks create a whirligig in the center, echoing the Whirligig blocks around them. Machine quilted.

Cardinal Block
Finished Size: 9" x 9"
Enlarge block on page 42 by 150% or use a grid with ¾" squares.

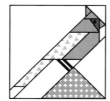

Whirligig Block
Finished Size: 6" x 6"
Four-patch block
1 square = 1½"

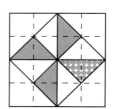

Materials: 44"-wide fabric

¾ yd. light green print for background
¾ yd. green print for bird perches and outer border
¼ yd. each of 3 red prints for birds and whirligigs
¾ yd. of 4th red print for birds, whirligigs, inner
  border, and binding
Small piece of black solid for bird faces
44" x 44" piece of batting
1¼" yds. backing fabric
Embroidery floss in black, white, and red

Directions

Cardinal Blocks

1. Cut and piece 4 Cardinal blocks, using the straight-line patchwork technique on pages 6–13. Make each bird from a different red print.
2. Embroider eye, using black embroidery floss; add a circle of red around the outside. Add a white highlight (page 20) using white embroidery floss. Embroider black legs.
3. Trim blocks to 9½" x 9½".

Whirligig Blocks

1. From background fabric, cut:
   32 squares, each 3⅞" x 3⅞"; cut once diagonally to yield 64 half-square triangles
   16 squares, each 4¼" x 4¼"; cut twice diagonally to yield 64 quarter-square triangles
2. From each of the 4 red print fabrics, cut 3 squares, each 4¼" x 4¼"; cut twice diagonally to yield 12 quarter-square triangles (48 total).
3. From the green print, cut 4 squares, each 4¼" x 4¼"; cut twice diagonally to yield 16 quarter-square triangles.
4. Piece 16 Whirligig blocks. Sew background quarter-square triangles to red and green quarter-square triangles to make squares.

Red   Green

Join 4 squares to make Whirligigs, using 3 squares with red triangles and 1 square with a green triangle.

Green

Add half-square triangles to each Whirligig as shown.

Quilt Top Assembly

1. Arrange the Cardinal blocks so that the birds circle around the center. Join the blocks into 2 rows of 2, then stitch the rows together.

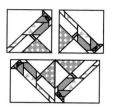

2. Arrange the Whirligig blocks around the Bird blocks, creating a pleasing balance of color and prints. Sew the Whirligig blocks together in vertical strips of 3 for each side of the birds, and horizontal strips of 5 for the top and bottom of the birds. Stitch Whirligig strips to the sides and then to the top and bottom of the birds.

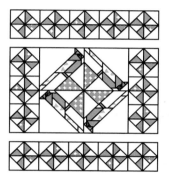

3. From the fourth red print, cut 4 inner border strips, each 1½" wide, across the fabric width. Measure the quilt across the center for the correct side border length as shown on page 21. Trim 2 inner border strips to this length and sew to opposite sides of the quilt top. Repeat with the remaining strips and sew to the top and bottom edges of the quilt top.
4. From the green print, cut 4 outer border strips, each 4½" wide, across the fabric width. Measure the quilt across the center for the correct side border length. Trim 2 outer border strips to this length and sew to opposite sides of the quilt top. Repeat with the remaining strips and sew to the top and bottom edges of the quilt top.

Quilt Finishing

1. Layer the quilt top with batting and backing; baste.
2. Quilt in the design of your choice.
3. Bind the quilt with 2½"-wide, straight-grain strips cut from the fourth red print. You will need approximately 152" of binding.

CANADA GOOSE BLOCK

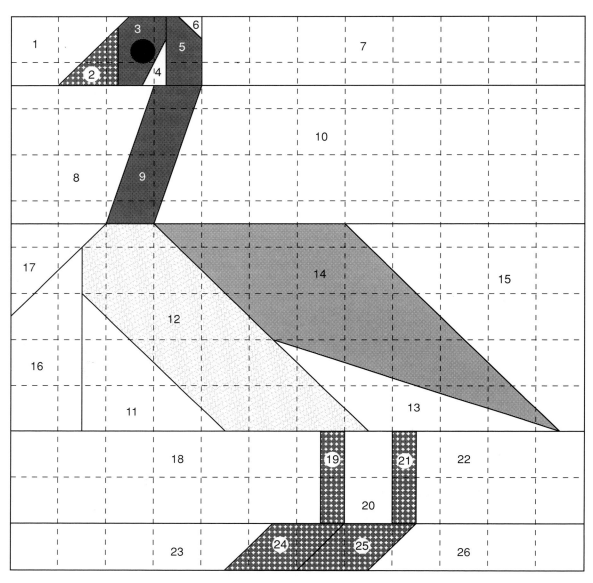

Block size shown: 6" x 6"   1 square = ½"

Size Options

To enlarge from the grid (12 x 12 squares):
    For 12" x 12" block, each square = 1"
To enlarge by photocopying:
    For 12" x 12" block, enlarge by 200% in 2 steps:
        1. 150%
        2. 133%

Follow this color key if you wish to make the Canada goose in its natural coloration.

▨ Beak, legs, and feet (dark gray) - 2, 19, 21, 24, 25

■ Head and neck (black) - 3, 5, 9

☐ Cheek and underbelly (white) - 4, 13

▫ Breast (gray) - 12

▦ Wing (brown) - 14

☐ Background - 1, 6, 7, 8, 10, 11, 15, 16, 17, 18, 20, 22, 23, 26

Piecing Order

A. 2 + 3 + 4
B. 5 + 6
C. 1 + (2-4) + (5-6) + 7

~~~~~~~~~~~~~~

D. 8 + 9 + 10

~~~~~~~~~~~~~~

E. 13 + 14
F. 11 + 12 + (13 -14) + 15
G. (11-15) + 16
H. (11-16) + 17

~~~~~~~~~~~~~~

I. 18 + 19 + 20 + 21 + 22

~~~~~~~~~~~~~~

J. 23 + 24 + 25 + 26

~~~~~~~~~~~~~~

K. (1-7) + (8-10) + (11-17) + (18-22) + (23-26)
L. Embroider eye.

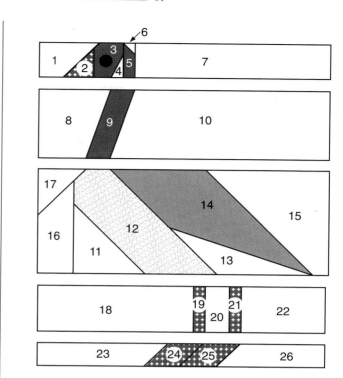

Major block sections

CANADA GOOSE QUILT

Canada Goose quilt, 39" x 39". A selection of antique-looking fabrics, made into simple borders, makes a small medallion quilt from the Canada Goose block. Hand quilted by Beth Miller.

Canada Goose Block

Finished Size: 12" x 12"
Enlarge block on page 46 by 200% or use a grid with 1" squares.

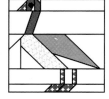

Materials: 44"-wide fabric

¾ yd. beige and maroon large-scale print for outer border

½ yd. beige print for background and border

Small pieces of solids in each of black and white for goose

Small pieces of prints in each of dark gray, white, brown, and light gray for goose

Small pieces of 9 assorted prints in maroon, rose, blue, tan, and blue/green for triangles and squares in pieced borders

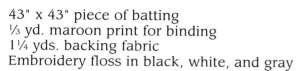

43" x 43" piece of batting
⅓ yd. maroon print for binding
1¼ yds. backing fabric
Embroidery floss in black, white, and gray

Directions

Canada Goose Block

1. Cut and piece the Canada Goose block, using the straight-line patchwork technique on pages 6–13. Make the goose's head and neck from black solid; cheek and underbelly from white print; beak, legs, and feet from dark gray print; breast from light gray print; and wing from brown print.
2. Embroider eye, using black embroidery floss, and add a white highlight (page 20). Embroider a circle of gray around the outside of the eye with a stem stitch.
3. Trim block to 12½" x 12½".

Quilt Top Assembly

1. From background fabric, cut:
   8 squares, each 2⅜" x 2⅜"; cut once diagonally to yield 16 half-square triangles
   7 squares, each 4¼" x 4¼"; cut twice diagonally to yield 28 quarter-square triangles
2. From assorted prints, cut:
   8 squares, each 2" x 2"
   9 squares, each 4¼" x 4¼"; cut twice diagonally to yield 36 quarter-square triangles
3. For pieced borders: Arrange print quarter-square and half-square triangles and corner squares around goose to create a pleasing balance of color. Piece triangles and squares into strips as shown and add to sides of goose, then to top and bottom edges.

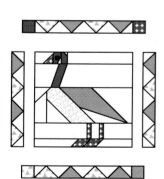 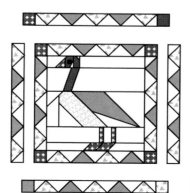

4. From background fabric, cut 2 border strips, each 2" x 18½". Sew to sides of quilt top. Cut 2 strips, each 2" x 21½". Sew to the top and bottom edges of the quilt top.

5. For pieced border: From assorted prints, cut 32 squares, each 3½" x 3½". Arrange squares around quilt top. Join side squares into vertical strips of 7 squares each and sew to sides of quilt top. Join squares at top and bottom into horizontal strips of 9 squares each and add to quilt top and bottom.

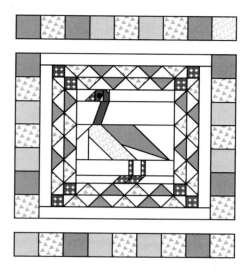

6. From beige and maroon print, cut 4 outer border strips, each 6½" wide, across the fabric width. Measure the quilt across the center for the correct side border length as shown on page 21. Trim 2 strips to this length and sew to opposite sides of the quilt top. Repeat with the remaining strips and sew to the top and bottom edges of the quilt top.

Quilt Finishing

1. Layer the quilt top with batting and backing; baste.
2. Quilt in the design of your choice.
   Suggestion: Outline quilt the goose, then quilt a diamond grid that follows the lines of the triangles. Outline the borders.
3. Bind the quilt with 2½"-wide, straight-grain strips cut from the maroon print. You will need approximately 156" of binding.

HUMMINGBIRD BLOCK

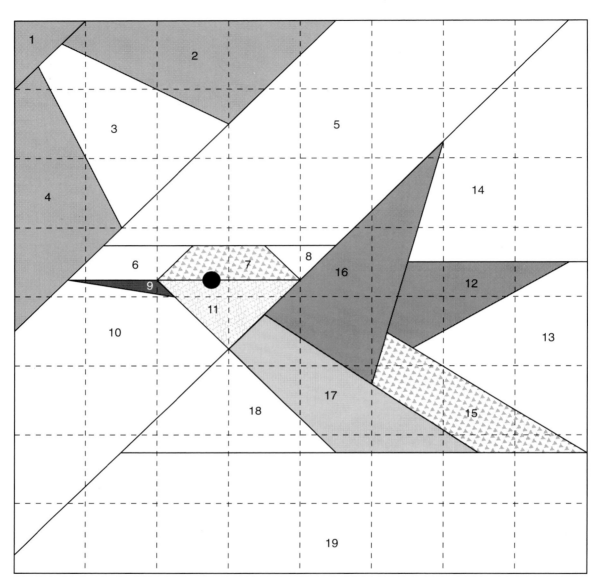

Block size shown: 6" x 6"   1 square = ¾"

Color photos on pages 15 and 52.

Size Options

To enlarge from the grid (8 x 8 squares):
    For 10" x 10" block, each square = 1¼"
    For 12" x 12" block, each square = 1½"
To enlarge by photocopying:
    For 10" x 10" block, enlarge by 167% in 2 steps:
        1. 150%
        2. 111%
    For 12" x 12" block, enlarge by 200% in 2 steps:
        1. 150%
        2. 133%

Follow this color key if you wish to make the hummingbird in its natural coloration.

- Flower (pink) - 1, 2, 4
- Head and back (green) - 7, 15
- Beak (gray) - 9
- Throat (ruby red) - 11
- Wings (gray/green) - 12, 16
- Breast (pale green) - 17
- Background - 3, 5, 6, 8, 10, 13, 14, 18, 19

Piecing Order

A. 2 + 3 + 4
B. 1 + (2-4)

C. 6 + 7 + 8
D. 9 + 10
E. (9-10) + 11
F. 5 + (6-8) + (9-11)

G. 12 + 13
H. (12-13) + 14
I. (12-14) + 15
J. (12-15) + 16
K. (12-16) + 17 + 18
L. (12-18) + 19

M. (1-4) + (5-11) + (12-19)
N. Appliqué eye.

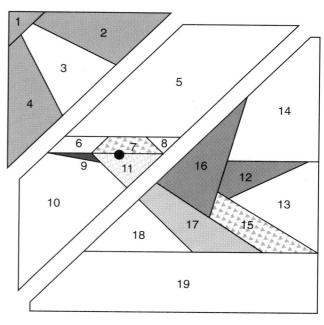

Major block sections

HUMMINGBIRD QUILT

Hummingbird quilt, 51" x 51". Hummingbirds circle around a stylized flower in a garden of chintz flowers. Hand quilted by Elizabeth Rose.

Hummingbird Block
Finished Size: 12" x 12"
Enlarge block on page 50
by 200% or use a grid
with 1" squares.

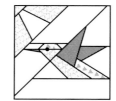

Materials: 44"-wide fabric
1¾ yds. pink-and-green floral print for background
1¼ yds. pink print for flower, border, and binding
½ yd. green print for birds and borders
Small pieces of print in each of pale green, green,
    bright pink, and gray for birds
Scrap of dark brown print for eyes
55" x 55" piece of batting
2¼" yds. backing fabric
Embroidery floss in white

Directions

Hummingbird Blocks

1. Cut and piece 4 Hummingbird blocks, using the straight-line patchwork technique on pages 6–13. Cut pieces for background from the length of the fabric to leave maximum length for cutting borders. Make bird's head and tail from green print, wings from second green print, throat from bright pink, breast from pale green, and beak from gray.
2. Appliqué eyes, using brown print, and embroider a white highlight (pages 19–20).
3. Trim blocks to 12½" x 12½".

Quilt Top Assembly

1. Arrange the Hummingbird blocks so that the birds circle around the center. Sew the blocks into 2 rows of 2, then join the rows together.

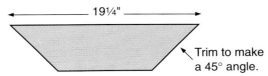

2. From background fabric, cut one 13¼" square; cut twice diagonally to yield 4 quarter-square triangles.
3. From the green print, cut 6 strips, each 2" wide, across the fabric width. Set 4 strips aside. Cut remaining 2 strips into 8 lengths, each 10¼". Using a right triangle or Bias Square cutting guide, trim both ends of each strip to make a 45° angle as shown.

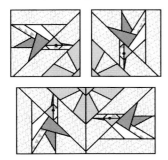

← 10¼" →
Trim to make a 45° angle.

4. From the pink print, cut 4 strips, each 5" wide, across the fabric width. Cut strips into 8 lengths, each 19¼". Using a right triangle or Bias Square cutting guide, trim both ends of each strip to make a 45° angle as shown.

← 19¼" →
Trim to make a 45° angle.

5. Sew green strips to pink strips. Then sew each background print triangle between 2 sets of strips to finish pieced border.

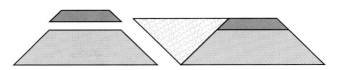

6. Sew pieced borders to birds, being careful not to sew into the seam allowances at each corner. Miter corners and press seams open (pages 21–22).

7. Trim remaining green print strips to 37¼". Using a right triangle or Bias Square cutting guide, trim both ends of each strip to make a 45° angle. Sew strips to edges of quilt and miter the corners.
8. From background print, cut 4 strips, each 6½" wide, from the length of the fabric. Cut strips into lengths of 52¼" (or length required when quilt is measured through the center), piecing as necessary. Sew strips to sides of quilt and miter the corners.

Quilt Finishing

1. Layer the quilt top with batting and backing; baste.
2. Quilt in the design of your choice.
   Suggestion: Outline quilt the birds and borders; quilt curved pattern on central flower; quilt trailing leaf pattern onto pink border; quilt pattern of concentric diamonds onto background.
3. Bind the quilt with 2½"-wide, straight-grain strips cut from the pink print. You will need approximately 204" of binding.

MALLARD DUCK BLOCK

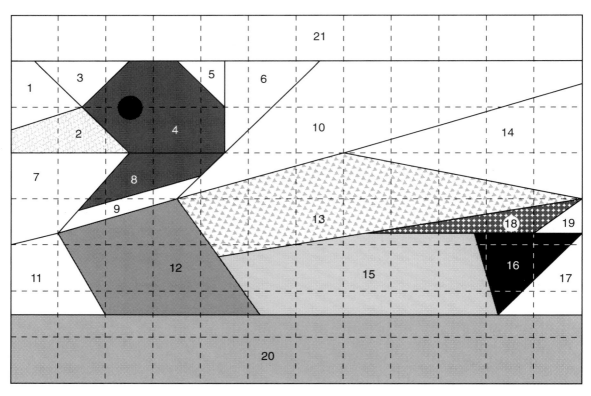

Block size shown: 4" x 6"   1 square = ½"

Color photos on pages 15 and 56.

Size Options

To enlarge from the grid (8 x 12 squares):
    For 6" x 9" block, each square = ¾"
    For 8" x 12" block, each square = 1"
To enlarge by photocopying:
    For 6" x 9" block, enlarge by 150%.
    For 8" x 12" block, enlarge by 200% in 2 steps:
        1. 150%
        2. 133%

Follow this color key if you wish to make the mallard duck in its natural coloration.

Bill (yellow) - 2
Head (green) - 4, 8
Neckband (white) - 9
Breast (rusty red) - 12
Wing (brown) - 13
Belly (cream) - 15
Tail (black) - 16
Wing edge (blue) - 18
Background - 1, 3, 5, 6, 7, 10, 11, 14, 17, 19, 21
Water - 20

Piecing Order

A. 1 + 2
B. 3 + 4 + 5
C. (1-2) + (3-5) + 6
D. 8 + 9
E. 7 + (8-9)
F. (1-6) + (7-9)
G. (1-9) + 10

~~~~~~~~

H. 13 + 14
 I. 15 + 16 + 17
 J. 18 + 19
K. (15-17) + (18-19)
 L. (13-14) + (15-19)
M. 11 + 12 + (13-19)

~~~~~~~~

N. (1-10) + (11-19) + 20 + 21
O. Appliqué eye.

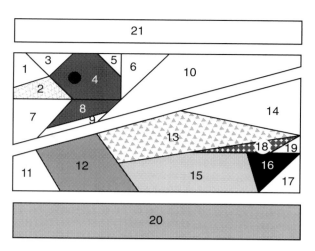

Major block sections

MALLARD DUCK QUILT

Duck quilt, 60" x 60". Duck blocks are alternated and incorporated into Duck and Duckling blocks and enhanced by a pieced border that echoes the shapes in the Duck and Duckling blocks. Hand quilted by Beth Miller.

Mallard Duck Block
Finished Size: 5½" x 12"
Enlarge block on page 54
by 200% or use a grid with
1" squares.
Omit pieces 20 and 21
when making this quilt.

Duck & Ducklings Block
Finished Size: 15" x 15"
Five-patch block
1 square = 3"

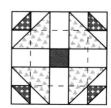

Materials: 44"-wide fabric

2 yds. beige print for background

1¼ yds. maroon print for large triangles in Duck and Ducklings blocks and pieced border

1 yd. blue print for triangles in blocks, pieced border, and binding

½ yd. green print for squares in Duck and Ducklings blocks and inner border

Small pieces of green, brown, black, yellow, dark red, blue, and cream prints for ducks

Scrap of white solid for duck's neckband

Scrap of black solid for duck's eyes

64" x 64" piece of batting

2¾ yds. backing fabric

Directions

Mallard Duck Blocks

1. Cut and piece 4 Mallard Duck blocks, using the straight-line patchwork technique on pages 6–13. Make the duck's head and neck from green print, neckband from white solid, beak from yellow print, breast from dark red print, belly from cream print, wing from brown print, wing edge from blue print, and tail from black print.
2. Appliqué black circles for eyes (page 19).
3. Trim each block to 6" x 12½".

Duck and Duckling Blocks

1. From the background fabric, cut:
   38 squares, each 3⅞" x 3⅞"; cut once diagonally to yield 76 half-square triangles (Set aside 16 triangles.)
   20 rectangles, each 3½" x 6½"
2. From green print, cut 5 squares, each 3½" x 3½".
3. From maroon print, cut 10 squares, each 6⅞" x 6⅞"; cut once diagonally to yield 20 half-square triangles.
4. From blue print, cut 18 squares, each 3⅞" x 3⅞"; cut once diagonally to yield 36 half-square triangles. (Set aside 16 triangles.)
5. Piece 5 Duck and Duckling blocks, following the piecing diagram below.

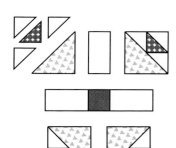
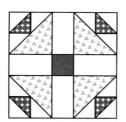

Quilt Top Assembly

1. From the background print, cut:
   8 strips, each 2" x 6½"
   4 strips, each 2" x 15½"
   4 strips, each 2½" x 15½"
   8 strips, each 3½" x 9½"
2. Sew the 2" x 6½" strips to the sides of each Mallard Duck block. Sew the 2" x 15½" strips to the top edges, and the 2½" x 15½" strips to the bottom edges of the Mallard Duck blocks.

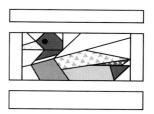

3. Using background and blue half-square triangles (set aside when cutting Duck and Ducklings blocks), piece 16 squares. Sew pieced squares to each end of the 3½" x 9½" strips of background print. Join these strips to the top and bottom edges of the Mallard Duck blocks, making them 15½" x 15½".

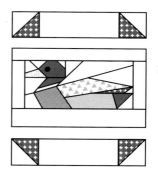

4. Sew Mallard Duck blocks and Duck and Duckling blocks into 3 rows of 3 blocks as shown in the quilt photo on page 56. Stitch rows together to make center of quilt.
5. From the green print, cut 5 inner border strips, each 2" wide, across the fabric width. Piece strips together to make a continuous border, pressing seams open, and cut 2 strips, each 45½" long. Sew border strips to opposite sides of quilt top. From remaining length, cut 2 strips, each 48½" long; sew to the top and bottom edges of the quilt top.
6. From the background print, cut 13 squares, each 7¼" x 7¼"; cut twice diagonally to yield 52 quarter-square triangles.

7. From maroon print, cut:
   4 squares, each 13¼" x 13¼"; cut twice diagonally to yield 16 quarter-square triangles
   2 squares, each 7¼" x 7¼"; cut twice diagonally
   to yield 8 quarter-square triangles
8. From blue print, cut:
   5 squares, each 7¼" x 7¼"; cut twice diagonally
   to yield 20 quarter-square triangles
9. Piece 4 border strips, following the piecing diagram below.

Make 4.

10. Sew border strips to each side of the quilt, stitch-
    ing to within ¼" of the corners; backstitch at
    each corner. Do not stitch into the seam allow-
    ances. Miter each corner and press seams open
    (pages 21–22).

Quilt Finishing

1. Layer the quilt top with batting and backing;
   baste.
2. Quilt in the design of your choice.
3. Bind the quilt with 3"-wide, straight-grain strips
   cut from the blue print. You will need approximately 240" of binding.

MOOSE BLOCK

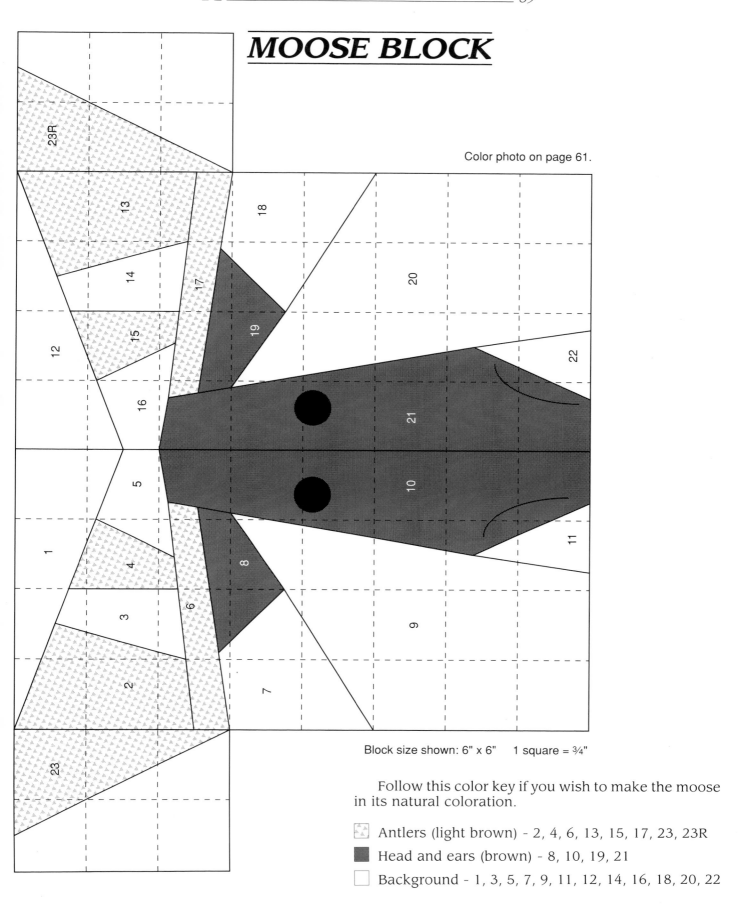

Color photo on page 61.

Block size shown: 6" x 6"   1 square = ¾"

Follow this color key if you wish to make the moose in its natural coloration.

Antlers (light brown) - 2, 4, 6, 13, 15, 17, 23, 23R

Head and ears (brown) - 8, 10, 19, 21

Background - 1, 3, 5, 7, 9, 11, 12, 14, 16, 18, 20, 22

Size Options

To enlarge from the grid:
   center Moose block (8 x 8 squares)
   outside antlers (3 x 2 squares)
   For 10" x 10" center block, each square = 1¼"
   For 12" x 12" center block, each square = 1½"
To enlarge by photocopying:
   For 10" x 10" center block, enlarge by 167% in 2
   steps:
      1. 150%
      2. 111%
   For 12" x 12" center block, enlarge by 200% in 2
   steps:
      1. 150%
      2. 133%

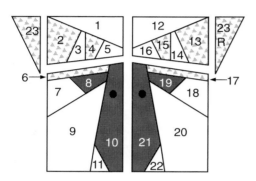

Major block sections

Piecing Order

A. 2 + 3 + 4 + 5
B. 1 + (2-5)

~~~~~

C. 7 + 8
D. 6 + (7-8) + 9
E. 10 + 11
F. (6-9) + (10-11)
G. (1-5) + (6-11)

~~~~~

H. 13 + 14 + 15 + 16
I. 12 + (13-16)

~~~~~

J. 18 + 19
K. 17 + (18-19) + 20
L. 21 + 22
M. (17-20) + (21-22)
N. (12-16) + (17-22)

~~~~~

O. (1-11) + (12-22)
    Press this central seam open. Sew pieces 23
    and 23R into adjoining blocks or borders.
P. Appliqué eyes; embroider or quilt nostrils.

MOOSE QUILT

Moose quilt, 45" x 45". Moose and nine–patch blocks alternate, with the moose's antlers extending into the neighboring blocks and borders to give the illusion of the enormous size of the moose antlers. Machine quilted.

Moose Block
Finished Size: 10" x 10"
(This measurement does not include the antler pieces, which are pieced into adjacent blocks or borders.)
Enlarge block on page 59 by 167% or use a grid with 1¼" squares.

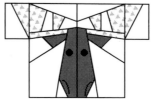

Nine-patch Block
Finished Size: 10" x 10"
1 square = 3⅜"

Materials: 44"-wide fabric

1⅓ yds. brown print for nine–patch blocks and outer border

1 yd. terracotta print for antlers and binding

⅔ yd. dark brown print for moose faces, ears, and inner border

½ yd. beige print for background of Moose blocks

¼ yd. beige plaid for nine–patch blocks

Scrap of black solid for moose's eyes

49" x 49" piece of batting

2¼ yds. backing fabric

Directions

Moose Blocks

1. Cut and piece 5 Moose blocks, using the straight-line patchwork technique on pages 6–13. Make moose face and ears from brown print, and antlers from terracotta print.
2. Using pieces 23 and 23R for the reverse (out-side antler piece on page 59), mark and cut out 5 antler pieces and 5 reverse antler pieces. Set these pieces aside.
3. Appliqué black circles for eyes (page 19).
4. Trim each block to 10½" x 10½".

Nine–patch Blocks

1. From the beige plaid, cut 16 squares, each 3⅞" x 3⅞".
2. From the brown print, cut 20 squares, each 3⅞" x 3⅞", from the lengthwise grain in order to preserve the length of the fabric for the outer border.
3. Piece 4 Nine–patch blocks.

4. Trim blocks to 10½" x 10½".
5. Use piece 23 to mark the corners of the nine-patch blocks where the antler pieces will be added. Mark around the antler piece (23 or 23R) on the wrong side of the nine-patch blocks, remembering to place it ¼" from the sides as shown.

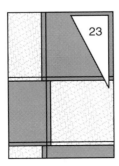

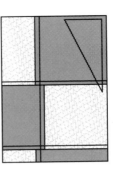

Antler piece marked on wrong side of nine-patch block

Two of the blocks have pieced antlers in each top corner, while the other two blocks have only one pieced antler, one in the top right corner, the other in the top left corner.

6. Trim marked corners of the nine-patch blocks, leaving a ¼"-wide seam allowance as shown.

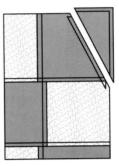

7. Pin and sew appropriate antler pieces to nine-patch blocks.

  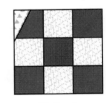

Make 2.   Make 1.   Make 1.

8. Trim corners to make blocks exactly 10½" x 10½".

Quilt Top Assembly

1. Sew blocks into 3 rows of 3 blocks each, alternating the Moose blocks and the nine-patch blocks as shown on page 63. Make sure that the antler pieces are correctly placed. Then sew the rows together.
2. From the dark brown print, cut 4 inner border strips, each 3" wide, across the fabric width. Trim these strips to make:

    2 strips, each 10½" long
    2 strips, each 20½" long
    2 strips, each 35½" long

3. Using pieces 23 and 23R for the reverse, mark around antler piece on the wrong side of the strips as follows: top right corner of a 10½" strip and a 20½" strip, and the top left corner of the

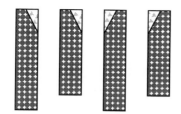

other 10½" and 20½" strips. See steps 5 and 6 on page 62 for marking and trimming corners. Pin and sew appropriate antler pieces to border strips.

Trim corner seam allowances so that strips are back to original size.

4. Join the 2 strips for the left side of the quilt together, then join the 2 strips for the right side of the quilt together. Sew the strips to each side of the quilt top.

5. Sew remaining inner border strips to top and bottom of the quilt.
6. From brown print, cut 4 outer border strips, each 5½" wide, from the length of the fabric. Measure the quilt through the center for the correct side border length as shown on page 21. Trim 2 inner border strips to this length and sew to opposite sides of the quilt top. Repeat measuring and trimming with the remaining strips and sew to the top and bottom edges of the quilt top.

Quilt Finishing

1. Layer the quilt top with batting and backing; baste.
2. Quilt in the design of your choice. Quilt nostrils onto moose.
3. Bind the quilt with 2½" wide, straight-grain strips cut from the terracotta print. You will need approximately 180" of binding.

ROBIN BLOCK

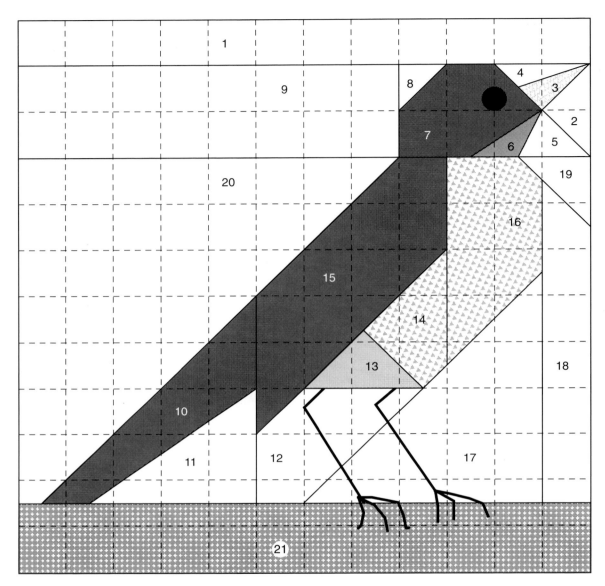

Block size shown: 6" x 6"   1 square = ½"

Color photos on pages 14 and 66.

Size Options

To enlarge from the grid (12 x 12 squares):
    For 9" x 9" block, each square = ¾"
    For 12" x 12" block, each square = 1"
To enlarge by photocopying:
    For 9" x 9" block, enlarge by 150%.
    For 12" x 12" block, enlarge by 200% in 2 steps:
        1. 150%
        2. 133%

Follow this color key if you wish to make the robin in its natural coloration.

☐ Beak (yellow) - 3

■ Head, wing and tail (brown) - 7, 10, 15

■ Neck (mottled brown) - 6

☐ Breast (reddish orange) - 14, 16

☐ Underbelly (white) - 13

☐ Background - 1, 2, 4, 5, 8, 9, 11, 12, 17, 18, 19, 20

▦ Ground (or background) - 21

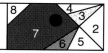

Piecing Order

A. 2 + 3 + 4
B. 5 + 6
C. (5-6) + 7 + 8
D. (2-4) + (5-8) + 9

∼∼∼∼∼∼

E. 10 + 11
F. 12 + 13 + 14
G. (12-14) + 15
H. (12-15) + 16
 I. (12-16) + 17
 J. (10 -11) + (12-17) + 18
K. (10-18) + 19 + 20

∼∼∼∼∼∼

L. 1 + (2-9) + (10-20) + 21
M. Embroider eye and legs.

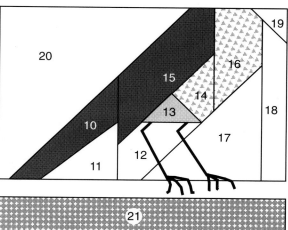

Major block sections

ROBIN IN SPRINGTIME QUILT

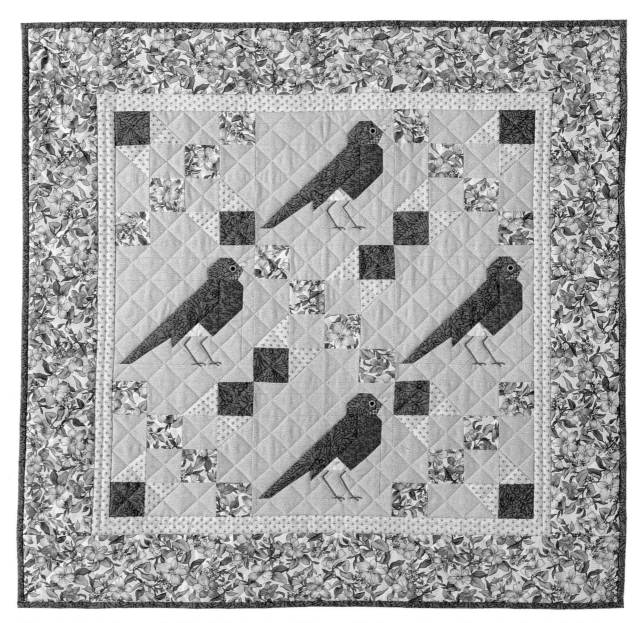

Robin in Springtime quilt, 39" x 39". Road to Oklahoma blocks combine with Robin blocks in fresh spring colors and prints. Machine quilted.

Robin Block
Finished Size: 9" x 9"
Enlarge block on page 64 by 150% or use a grid with ¾" squares.

Road to Oklahoma Block
Finished Size: 9" x 9"
Four-patch block
1 square = 2¼"

Materials: 44"-wide fabric

¾ yd. floral print for Road to Oklahoma blocks and outer border
⅔ yd. green print for robins' bodies, Road to Oklahoma blocks, and binding
⅔ yd. pale green print for background of robins and Road to Oklahoma blocks
½ yd. yellow print for robins' beaks, Road to Oklahoma blocks, and inner border
⅛ yd. coral pink print for robin's breasts
Small piece of cream print for robin's underbelly
Scrap of green check for robins' throats
43" x 43" piece of batting
1¼ yds. backing fabric
Embroidery floss in brown, dark green, and pink

Directions

Robin Blocks

1. Cut and piece 4 Robin blocks, using the straight-line patchwork technique on pages 6–13. Make robin's head, wing, and tail from green print; breast from coral pink; throat from green check; beak from yellow print; and underbelly from cream print.
2. Embroider eyes with dark green centers and outer circle of pink (page 20). Embroider brown legs and feet.
3. Trim each block to 9½" x 9½".

Road to Oklahoma Blocks

1. From the background fabric, cut:
   30 squares, each 2¾" x 2¾"
   10 squares, each 3⅛" x 3⅛"; cut once diagonally to yield 20 half-square triangles
2. From the floral print, cut 20 squares, each 2¾" x 2¾".
3. From the yellow print, cut 10 squares, each 3⅛" x 3⅛"; cut once diagonally to yield 20 half-square triangles.
4. Sew background and yellow print half-square triangles together to make 20 pieced squares.
5. Join background and floral squares with pieced squares into rows and join rows, following the piecing diagram below.

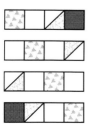

Quilt Top Assembly

1. Sew the Robin and Road to Oklahoma blocks into 3 rows of 3 blocks each as shown in the quilt photo on page 66. Then join the rows together.
2. From the yellow print, cut 4 inner border strips, each 2" wide, across the fabric width. Measure the quilt through the center for the correct side border length as shown on page 21. Trim 2 inner border strips to this length and sew to opposite sides of the quilt top. Repeat measuring and trimming with the remaining strips and sew to the top and bottom edges of the quilt top.
3. From the floral print, cut 4 outer border strips, each 5" wide, across the fabric width. Measure the quilt through the center for the correct side border length. Trim 2 inner border strips to this length and sew to opposite sides of the quilt top. Repeat measuring, trimming, and sewing with the remaining strips and sew to the top and bottom edges of the quilt top.

Quilt Finishing

1. Layer the quilt top with batting and backing; baste.
2. Quilt in the design of your choice.
3. Bind the quilt with 2½"-wide, straight-grain strips cut from the green print. You will need approximately 156" of binding.

SQUIRREL BLOCK

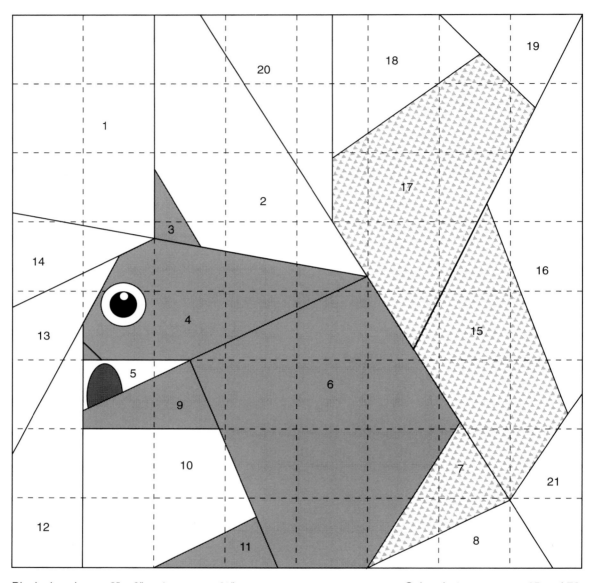

Block size shown: 6" x 6"   1 square = ¾"   Color photos on pages 15 and 70.

Size Options

To enlarge from the grid (8 x 8 squares):
    For 10" x 10" block, each square = 1¼"
    For 12" x 12" block, each square = 1½"
To enlarge by photocopying:
    For 10" x 10" block, enlarge by 167% in 2 steps:
        1. 150%
        2. 111%
    For 12" x 12" block, enlarge by 200% in 2 steps:
        1. 150%
        2. 133%

Follow this color key if you wish to make the squirrel in its natural coloration.

Squirrel body (brown) - 3, 4, 6, 9, 11

Tail (brown print) - 7, 15, 17

Background - 1, 2, 5, 8, 10, 12, 13, 14, 16, 18, 19, 20, 21

Piecing Order

A. 2 + 3
B. 1 + (2-3)

∽∽∽∽∽∽∽

C. 4 + 5
D. 6 + 7 + 8
E. 9 + 10 + 11
F. (6-8) + (9-11)
G. (4-5) + (6-11)
H. (4-11) + 12
 I. (4-12) + 13
J. (4-13) + 14

∽∽∽∽∽∽∽

K. (1-3) + (4-14)

∽∽∽∽∽∽∽

L. 15 + 16
M. 17 + 18
N. (17-18) + 19
O. (17-19) + 20
P. (15-16) + (17-20) + 21

∽∽∽∽∽∽∽

Q. (1-14) + (15-21)
R. Appliqué eye and nut in squirrel's paws.

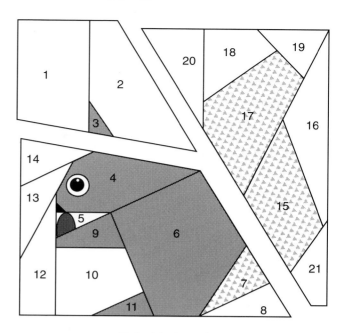

Major block sections

TARTAN SQUIRRELS QUILT

Tartan Squirrels quilt, 35" x 35". Squirrel blocks combine with Square in a Square blocks in bright primary-colored tartans and solids. Machine quilted.

Squirrel Block
Finished Size: 10" x 10"
Enlarge block shown on page 68 by 167% or use a
grid with 1¼" squares.

Small Square in a Square Blocks
Finished Size: 2½" x 2½"
Four-patch block
1 square = 1¼"

Large Square in a Square Blocks
Finished Size: 5" x 5"
Four-patch block
1 square = 2½"

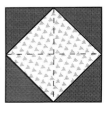

Materials: 44"-wide fabric

1⅔ yds. navy blue solid for background, sashing, inner border, binding, and squirrels' eyes

¼ yd. each of 6 assorted tartans in red, blue, green, and yellow for squirrel tails, nuts, and pieced squares in center and border

Small pieces of red, blue, yellow, and green solids for squirrel bodies

39" x 39" piece of batting

1¼ yds. backing fabric

Directions

Squirrel Blocks

1. Cut and piece 4 Squirrel blocks, using the straight-line patchwork technique on pages 6–13. Be sure to cut 2 squirrels in a reverse image by using the templates face up when you mark the fabric. Make 1 squirrel each in red, blue, yellow, and green solid, with matching-colored tartan tails and nuts.
2. Appliqué eyes by making a circle of navy solid (page 19). Appliqué nuts from scraps of tartan prints.
3. Trim each block to 10½" x 10½".

Small Square in a Square Blocks

1. From navy blue solid, cut 20 squares, each 1¾" x 1¾". From 5 of the tartan fabrics, cut 1 square, 3" x 3" (5 squares total).
2. Press navy squares in half diagonally and open out (the crease provides an accurate sewing line). With right sides together, place a creased navy square on top of one corner of a tartan square and match the outside corner precisely. Sew on the crease line. Trim away excess fabric and press open.

Crease line

Repeat this process with diagonally opposite corner, then remaining 2 corners. Make 5 blocks, each 3" x 3".

Large Square in a Square Blocks

1. From the navy blue solid, cut 96 squares, each 3" x 3". From each of the 6 tartan fabrics, cut 4 squares, each 5½" x 5½" (24 squares total).
2. Following the same procedure as described for small Square in a Square blocks, make 24 blocks, each 5½" x 5½".

Quilt Top Assembly

1. From navy blue solid, cut 4 sashing strips, each 3" x 8".
2. Sew a small tartan Square in a Square block to one end of each of the 4 sashing strips.

3. Join 2 pieced sashing strips with a single small Square in a Square block in the center. Piece sashing strips and Squirrel blocks, following the piecing diagram below.

4. From navy blue solid, cut 4 inner border strips, each 1¾" wide, across the fabric width. Cut 2 strips, each 23" long, and sew to opposite sides of the quilt top. Cut remaining 2 strips, each 25½" long, and sew to the top and bottom edges of the quilt top.
5. Arrange large Square in a Square blocks around the squirrels, creating a pleasing balance of tartan plaids. Sew blocks together in vertical strips of 5 for each side of the quilt and horizontal strips of 7 for the top and bottom of the quilt. Add outer border to sides, then to top and bottom of quilt as shown.

Quilt Finishing

1. Layer the quilt top with batting and backing; baste.
2. Quilt in the design of your choice.
3. Bind the quilt with 3"-wide, straight-grain strips cut from the navy background fabric. You will need approximately 140" of binding.

SWALLOW BLOCK

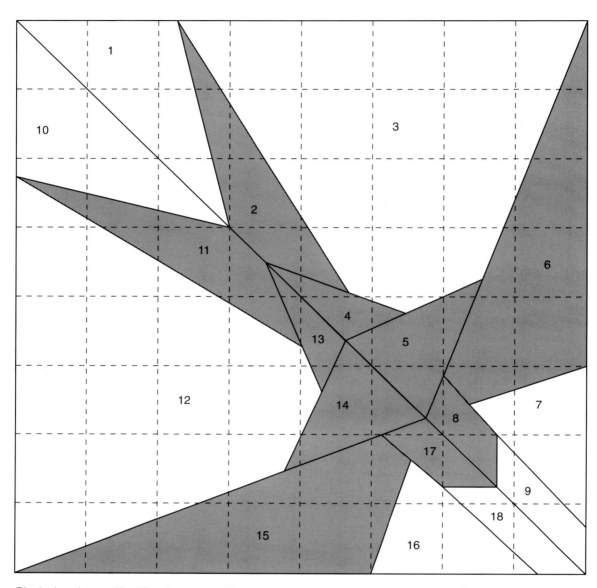

Block size shown: 6" x 6"   1 square = ¾"

Color photo on page 74.

Size Options

To enlarge from the grid (8 x 8 squares):
  For 8" x 8" block, each square = 1"
  For 10" x 10" block, each square = 1¼"
  For 12" x 12" block, each square = 1½"
To enlarge by photocopying:
  For 8" x 8" block, enlarge by 133%.
  For 10" x 10" block, enlarge by 167% in 2 steps:
      1. 150%
      2. 111%
  For 12" x 12" block, enlarge by 200% in 2 steps:
      1. 150%
      2. 133%

Follow this color key if you wish to make the swallow in its natural coloration.

Swallow (dark blue) - 2, 4, 5, 6, 8, 11, 13, 14, 15, 17

Background - 1, 3, 7, 9, 10, 12, 16, 18

Piecing Order

A. 1 + 2 + 3
B. (1-3) + 4
C. (1-4) + 5
D. 6 + 7
E. 8 + 9
F. (6-7) + (8-9)
G. (1-5) + (6-9)

≈≈≈≈≈≈

H. 10 + 11 + 12
I. (10-12) + 13
J. (10-13) + 14
K. 15 + 16
L. 17 + 18
M. (15-16) + (17-18)
N. (10-14) + (15-18)

≈≈≈≈≈≈

O. (1-9) + (10-18)
Press this seam open.

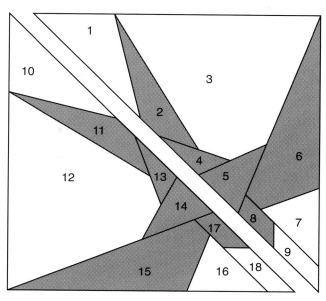

Major block sections

FLOCK OF SWALLOWS QUILT

Flock of Swallows quilt, 40" x 40". Swallow blocks circle around the center of a background created by Flock of Geese blocks. Machine quilted.

Swallow Block
Finished Size: 8" x 8"
Enlarge block on page 72
by 133% or use
a grid with 1" squares.

Flock of Geese Blocks
Finished Size: 8" x 8"
Four-patch block
1 square = 2"

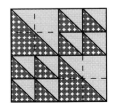

Materials: 44"-wide fabric

1¼ yds. light blue print for background
⅔ yd. royal blue print for birds and binding
¼ yd. each of 6 assorted purple, royal blue, turquoise, and magenta prints for Flock of Geese blocks and pieced borders
44" x 44" piece of batting
1¼ yds. backing fabric

Directions

Swallow Blocks

1. Cut and piece 4 Swallow blocks, using the straight-line patchwork technique on pages 6–13.
2. Trim each block to 8½" x 8½".

Flock of Geese Blocks

1. From background fabric, cut:
   30 squares, each 4⅞" x 4⅞"; cut once diagonally to yield 60 half-square triangles. Set aside 36 triangles for border.
   48 squares each 2⅞" x 2⅞"; cut once diagonally to yield 96 half-square triangles.
2. From each of the 6 assorted prints, cut:
   3 squares, each 4⅞" x 4⅞"; cut once diagonally to yield 6 half-square triangles (72 total). Set aside 4 triangles from each print for border.
   4 squares, each 2⅞" x 2⅞"; cut once diagonally to yield 8 half-square triangles (96 total).
3. Piece 12 Flock of Geese blocks, following the piecing diagram below.

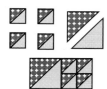

Quilt Top Assembly

1. Arrange Swallow blocks so that the birds fly around the center. Add Flock of Geese blocks around the center to create a pleasing balance of color and print, rotating the blocks as shown below. Sew the blocks into horizontal rows, then sew the rows together.

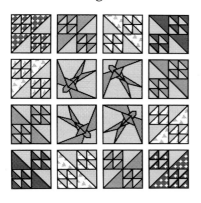

2. From remaining large half-square triangles (using only 3 triangles of each print), piece print triangles to background triangles to make 36 pieced squares. (You will have 1 triangle from each print left over.)
3. Sew 8 pieced squares together for the side borders and 10 pieced squares together for the top and bottom borders as shown. Notice the orientation of the background triangles.

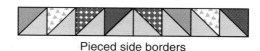

Pieced side borders

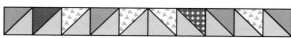

Pieced top and bottom borders

4. Join pieced borders to sides of quilt top and then to top and bottom.

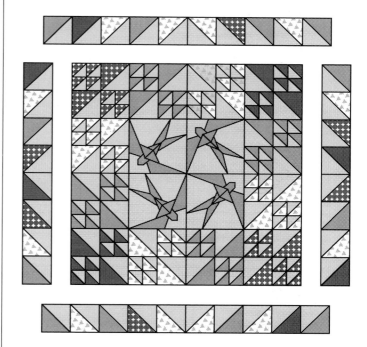

Quilt Finishing

1. Layer the quilt top with batting and backing; baste.
2. Quilt in the design of your choice.
3. Bind the quilt with 2½"-wide, straight-grain strips cut from the royal blue print. You will need approximately 160" of binding.

RACCOON BLOCK

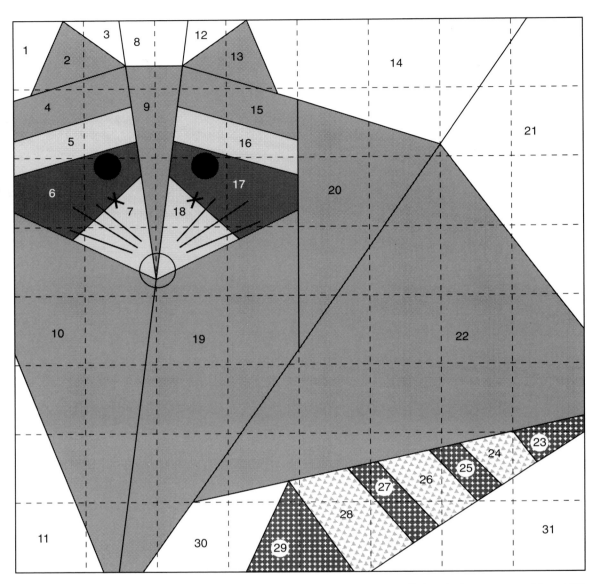

Block size shown: 6" x 6"   1 square = ¾"

Color photos on pages 14 and 78.

Size Options

To enlarge from the grid (8 x 8 squares):
    For 10" x 10" block, each square = 1¼"
    For 12" x 12" block, each square = 1½"
To enlarge by photocopying:
    For 10" x 10 block, enlarge by 167% in 2 steps:
        1. 150%
        2. 111%
    For 12" x 12" block, enlarge by 200% in 2 steps:
        1. 150%
        2. 133%

Follow this color key if you wish to make the raccoon in its natural coloration.

- Body and head (Gray/brown) - 2, 4, 9, 10, 13, 15, 19, 20, 22
- Nose and stripes above eyes (light gray) - 5, 7, 16, 18
- Eye patches (black) - 6, 17
- Dark tail stripes (dark brown) - 23, 25, 27, 29
- Light tail stripes (yellow) - 24, 26, 28
- Background - 1, 3, 8, 11, 12, 14, 21, 30, 31

Piecing Order

A. 1 + 2 + 3
B. 4 + 5 + 6 + 7
C. (1-3) + (4-7)
D. 8 + 9
E. (1-7) + (8-9)
F. (1-9) + 10 + 11

~~~~~~~~~~

G. 12 + 13 + 14
H. 15 + 16 + 17 + 18
I. (15-18) + 19
J. (15-19) + 20
K. (12-14) + (15-20)

~~~~~~~~~~

L. 21 + 22
M. 23 + 24 + 25 + 26 + 27 + 28 + 29
N. (23-29) + 30 + 31
O. (21-22) + (23-31)

~~~~~~~~~~

P. (1-11) + (12-20) + (21-31)
Q. Appliqué eyes and nose; embroider whiskers.

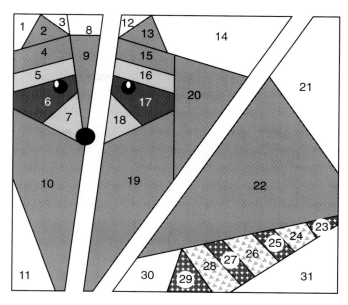

Major block sections

RACCOON QUILT

Raccoon quilt, 28½" x 28½". A border of simple triangles, made from a berry print, makes a background for the raccoon. Machine quilted.

Raccoon Block
Finished Size: 10" x 10"
Enlarge block on page 76 by 167% or use a grid with 1¼" squares.

Materials: 44"-wide fabric
¾ yd. red-and-green print for pieced triangles and outer border
½ yd. white print for background
¼ yd. brown print for raccoon body
¼ yd. green print for inner border
¼ yd. red print for binding
Small pieces of black, light gray, mustard, and dark brown prints for eye patches, face, and tail
Scrap of black solid for eyes and nose
43" x 43" piece of batting

1¼ yds. backing fabric
Embroidery floss in white

Directions

Raccoon Block

1. Cut and piece 1 Raccoon block, using the straight-line patchwork technique on pages 6–13. Make raccoon body and head from brown print, nose and strips above eyes from light gray print, eye patches from black print, and tail from combination of dark brown and mustard prints.
2. Appliqué eyes and nose by making circles of black solid (page 19). With white floss, embroider a highlight on eye, and whiskers on face (page 20).
3. Trim block to 10½" x 10½".

Quilt Top Assembly

1. From background fabric, cut:
   1 square, 11¼" x 11¼"; cut twice diagonally to yield 4 quarter-square triangles
   12 squares, each 3⅜" x 3⅜"; cut once diagonally to yield 24 half-square triangles
2. From red-and-green print, cut 20 squares, each 3⅜" x 3⅜"; cut once diagonally to yield 40 half-square triangles.
3. Join large quarter-square triangles of background fabric to sides of the Raccoon block in the order shown.

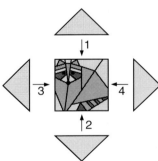

4. Piece the background half-square triangles to the red-and-green print half-square triangles to make 24 pieced squares.
5. Join pieced squares into rows, with extra red-and-green print triangles at end of each row as shown. Sew rows together to make 4 large pieced triangles.

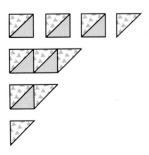

6. Join pieced triangles to Raccoon block.

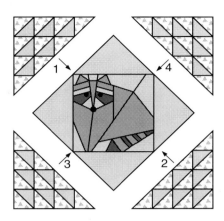

7. From green print, cut 2 inner border strips, each 1¾" x 20½", and sew to the sides of the quilt top. Cut 2 strips, each 1¾" x 23"; sew to top and bottom edges of the quilt top.
8. From red-and-green print, cut 2 squares, each 3⅞" x 3⅞"; cut once diagonally to yield 4 half-square triangles.
9. From white print for background, cut 2 squares, each 3⅞" x 3⅞"; cut once diagonally to yield 4 half-square triangles.
10. Piece background half-square triangles to the print half-square triangles to make 4 pieced corner squares.
11. From red-and-green print, cut 4 outer border strips, each 3½" wide, across the fabric width. Trim strips to make 4 lengths, each 23". Join 2 strips to opposite sides of the quilt top.
12. Sew pieced corner squares to each end of the remaining 2 strips.

13. Sew border strips to top and bottom edges of the quilt top as shown in photo on page 78.

Quilt Finishing

1. Layer the quilt top with batting and backing; baste.
2. Quilt in the design of your choice.
3. Bind the quilt with 2½"-wide, straight-grain strips cut from the red print. You will need approximately 114" of binding.

BALD EAGLE BLOCK

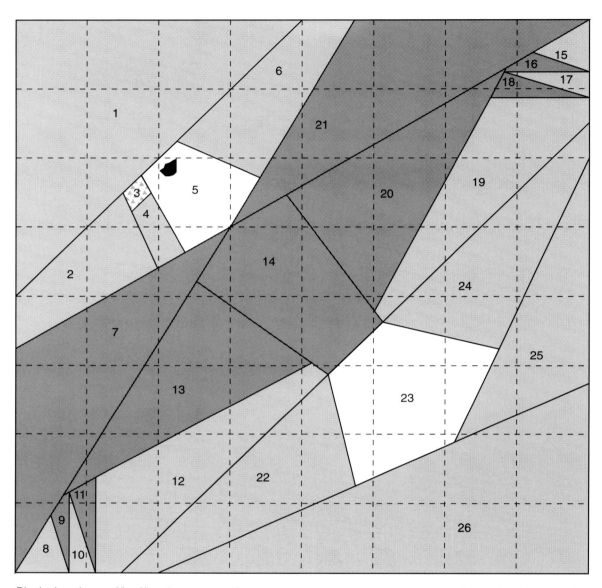

Block size shown: 6" x 6"   1 square = ¾"

Color photo on page 82.

Size Options

To enlarge from the grid (8 x 8 squares):
   For 12" x 12" block, each square = 1½"
   For 16" x 16" block, each square = 2"
To enlarge by photocopying:
   For 12" x 12" block, enlarge by 200% in 2 steps:
      1. 150%
      2. 133%
   For 16" x 16" block, enlarge by 267% in 3 steps:
      1. 150%
      2. 133%
      3. 133%

Follow this color key if you wish to make the bald eagle in its natural coloration.

Beak (yellow) - 3

Head and tail (white) - 5, 23

Body and wings (brown) - 7, 9, 11, 13, 14, 16, 18, 20, 21

Background - 1, 2, 4, 6, 8, 10, 12, 15, 17, 19, 22, 24, 25, 26

Piecing Order

A. 3 + 4
B. 2 + (3-4) + 5 + 6
C. 1 + (2-6) + 7

~~~~~~~

D. 8 + 9 + 10 + 11 + 12
E. (8-12) + 13
F. (8-13) + 14
G. 15 + 16 + 17 + 18 + 19
H. (15-19) + 20
 I. (8-14) + (15-20)
J. (8-20) + 21

~~~~~~~

K. 22 + 23 + 24
L. (22-24) + 25
M. (22-25) + 26

~~~~~~~

N. (1-7) + (8-21) + (22-26)
O. Embroider eye.

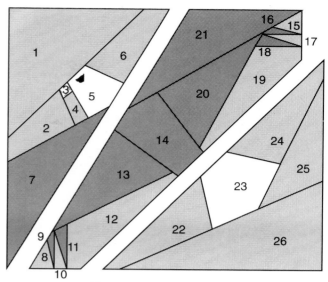

Major block sections

EAGLE IN THE MOUNTAINS QUILT

Eagle in the Mountains quilt, 53½" x 53½". The eagle is the focus in the center of a pattern of Delectable Mountains blocks, expressing the majesty of the bald eagle flying free in the wilds of the Rocky Mountains. Hand quilted.

Eagle Block
Finished Size: 12" x 12"
(set on point)
Enlarge block on page 80
by 200% or use a grid with
1½" squares.

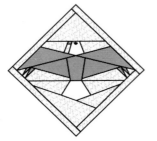

Delectable Mountains Blocks
Finished Size: 7½" x 7½"
Five-patch block
1 square = 1½"

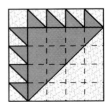

Materials: 44"-wide fabric

3 yds. light blue print for background and outer border
2½ yds. blue print for eagle, Delectable Mountains blocks, pieced border, and binding
⅔ yd. white solid for eagle, Delectable Mountains blocks, and inner border
58" x 58" piece of batting
2½ yds. backing fabric
Embroidery floss in dark yellow and black

Directions

Eagle Blocks

1. Cut and piece 1 Eagle block, using the straight-line patchwork technique on pages 6–13. Make body, wings, and beak from blue print, and head and tail from white solid.
2. Embroider yellow eye with black center, outline, and brow (page 20).
3. Trim block to 12½" x 12½".
4. From background print, cut 2 sashing strips, each 2" x 12½", and sew to opposite sides of the Eagle block. Cut 2 sashing strips, each 2" x 15½". Sew to the remaining sides of the Eagle block.

Delectable Mountains Blocks

1. Using background fabric and blue print, make 128 bias squares, each 2" x 2" (page 18).
2. Using background fabric and white solid, make 32 bias squares, each 2" x 2".
3. From background fabric, cut:
   20 squares, each 2" x 2"
   10 squares, each 6⅞" x 6⅞"; cut once diagonally to yield 20 half-square triangles
4. From blue print, cut 10 squares, each 6⅞" x 6⅞"; cut once diagonally to yield 20 half-square triangles.
5. Piece 20 Delectable Mountains blocks as shown to make 16 blocks with blue print peaks, and 4 blocks with white solid peaks.

Make 16.   Make 4.

Quilt Top Assembly

1. From background fabric, cut 8 squares, each 8⅜" x 8⅜"; cut once diagonally to yield 16 half-square triangles.
2. Arrange the Delectable Mountains blocks around the Eagle block in diagonal rows, placing the blocks with the white peaks at the center edge of each side. Place triangles around the edges of the quilt, between the Delectable Mountains blocks.

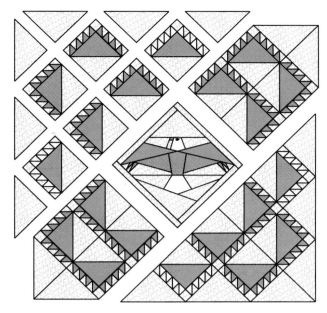

3. Sew the edge triangles and blocks into diagonal rows as shown. Join rows together.
4. From white solid, cut 5 inner border strips, each 2" wide, across the fabric width. Measure the quilt across the center for the correct border length as shown on page 21. Trim 2 strips to this length and sew to opposite sides of the quilt top. Repeat measuring and use remaining strips to create lengths required. Sew strips to top and bottom edges of the quilt top.
5. Using background fabric and blue print, cut 88 bias squares, each 2½" x 2½" (page 18). Join bias squares into 8 strips of 11 bias squares each, rotating the triangles as shown to make the middle border. You should have 4 pairs of pieced strips.

6. From background fabric, cut 4 rectangles, each 2" x 2½". Measure the quilt through the center to find the correct length for the border strips. Sew the rectangles between each pair of pieced strips, adjusting the size of the center rectangle so that the pieced border is the correct length. Sew 2 completed border strips to opposite sides of the quilt top.

Adjust border length here.

7. From background fabric, cut 4 squares, each 2½" x 2½". Sew the squares to the ends of remaining pieced border strips, then sew to top and bottom edges of the quilt top.

Adjust border length here.

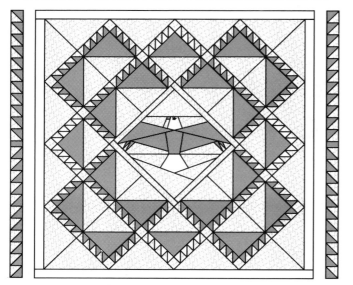

Quilt Finishing

1. Layer the quilt top with batting and backing; baste.
2. Quilt in the design of your choice.
3. Bind the quilt with 2½"-wide, straight-grain strips cut from the blue print. You will need approximately 214" of binding.

8. From background fabric, cut 6 outer border strips, each 2½" wide, across the fabric width. Measure the quilt across the center to find the correct border length. Joining strips to make this length, make 2 strips and sew to opposite sides of the quilt top. Repeat measuring and use remaining strips for the top and bottom edges of the quilt top. Sew strips to quilt top.

OWL BLOCK

Follow this color key if you wish to make the owl in its natural coloration.

■ Top of head and wings (dark brown) - 5, 7, 14, 27, 31

▨ Face (light brown) - 3, 10, 17, 21

▨ Side of head (brown) - 2, 4, 20, 22

□ Neck and underbelly (cream) - 9, 16, 25, 29

▨ Beak (very dark brown) - 11, 18

▨ Breast and tail (beige) - 8, 15, 26, 30

■ Branch (brown) - 24

□ Background - 1, 6, 12, 13, 19, 23, 28, 32

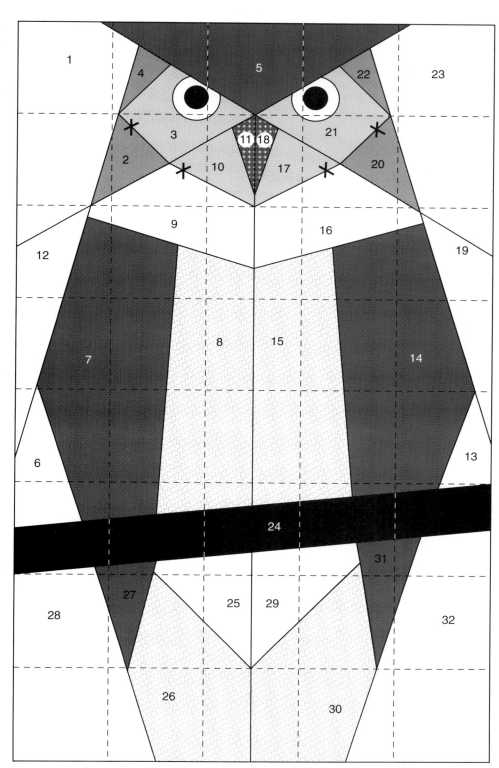

Size Options

To enlarge from the grid (8 x 5 squares):

For 12" x 7½" block, each square = 1½"

For 16" x 10" block, each square = 2"

To enlarge by photocopying:

For 12" x 7½" block, enlarge by 150%.

For 16" x 10" block, enlarge by 200% in 2 steps:

1. 150%
2. 133%

Block size shown: 8" x 5"   1 square = 1"   Color photo on page 87.

Piecing Order

A. 2 + 3 + 4
B. 1 + (2-4)
C. (1-4) + 5

D. 6 + 7 + 8
E. (6-8) + 9 + 10 + 11
F. (6-11) + 12
G. 13 + 14 + 15
H. (13-15) + 16 + 17 + 18
I. (13-18) + 19
J. (6-12) + (13-19)
   Press this seam open.

K. 20 + 21 + 22
L. (20-22) + 23

M. (6-19) + (20-23)

N. 25 + 26
O. (25-26) + 27
P. (25-27) + 28
Q. 29 + 30
R. (29-30) + 31
S. (29-31) + 32
T. (25-28) + (29-32)
   Press this seam open.
U. 24 + (25-32)

V. (1-5) + (6-23) + (24-32)
W. Appliqué yellow eyes with black centers.

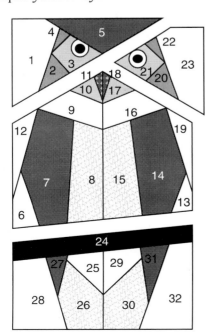

Major block sections

OWL QUILT

Owl quilt, 40½" x 31½". A variety of brown prints gives richness to a set of horned owls. Machine quilted.

Owl Block
Finished Size: 12" x 7½"
Enlarge block on page 85
by 150% or use a grid
with 1½" squares.

Materials: 44"-wide fabric

The best effect is gained when each owl is made from a different group of fabrics. For each owl, you will need small pieces of 5 brown prints in a range of values from dark to light brown; brown for the branch, dark brown for head and wings, medium brown for sides of face, and 2 light browns for face and breast. These brown prints are also used to make the triangles in the pieced border.

However, if you do not have access to such a

wide variety of brown prints, use the following quantities for making each owl the same: ¼ yd. brown for branches; ¼ yd. dark brown for heads and wings; ¼ yd. medium brown for sides of face; ¼ yd. light brown for face; and ¼ yd. light brown for breasts and tails.

Small pieces of 4 beige prints for owl neck and underbelly or if all owls are the same, ⅛ yd. of beige print

1¼ yds. black print for background, pieced outer border, and binding

½ yd. brown print for sashing and inner border

Small piece of black print for beaks

Scraps of yellow and black solid for eyes

45" x 35" piece of batting

1¼ yds. backing fabric

Directions

Owl Blocks

1. Cut and piece 4 Owl blocks, using the straight-line patchwork technique on pages 6–13. Be sure to make 2 owls reversed by using the templates face up when you mark the fabric.

2. Appliqué eyes by making a circle of yellow solid with a circle of black solid in the center (page 19). When placing the yellow circle on the face, fold a little of the yellow circle under so that the black center of the eye touches the top of the owl's head (piece #5).

3. Trim each block to 12½" x 8".

4. From background fabric, cut 8 strips, each 2" x 12½". Sew strips to opposite sides of the Owl blocks.

5. From fabric for branches, cut 8 strips, each 1¼" x 4". (For each branch of the Owl blocks, there should be 2 matching strips.)

6. Working on the wrong side of each block, draw 2 parallel lines, ¾" apart, at an angle through the side strips of each block, making the angles up or down as shown. Remove a couple of inches of stitches where the pieces of branches will meet, then cut down the center between your parallel lines, making ¼" seam allowances. Sew the short strips of branch fabrics into the space created, then re-sew the side seams. Trim side seam allowances of extra fabric created by the branch strips.

7. Arrange Owl blocks as shown below, with owls reversed in alternate blocks. From background fabric, cut 4 strips, each 2" x 11". Sew strips to the top and bottom of Owl blocks at the left-hand side of the quilt.

8. From background fabric, cut:
   2 strips, each 1¼" x 11"
   2 strips, each 2¾" x 11"

   Sew strips above and below each Owl block at the right-hand side of the quilt as shown below. This variation adds some interest by offsetting the blocks slightly. Owl blocks should measure 15½" x 11".

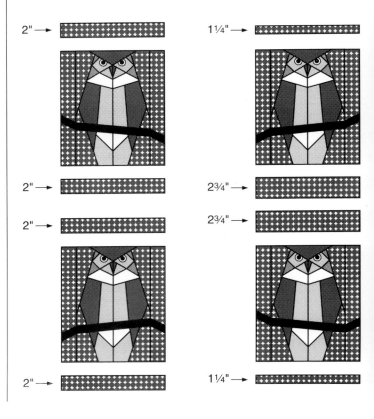

Quilt Top Assembly

1. From brown print for sashing, cut 6 strips, each 2" x 15½". Sew sashing strips between and on either side of the Owl blocks as shown below. Place Owl blocks facing in opposite directions next to each other.
2. From brown print, cut 3 strips, each 2" x 26". Join rows of owls together, with sashing strips above, between, and below rows.

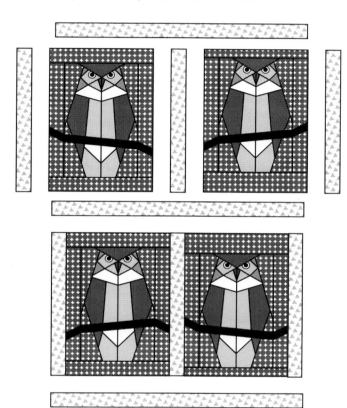

3. From brown prints, cut 20 squares, each 3⅞" x 3⅞"; cut once diagonally to yield 40 half-square triangles.
4. From background fabric, cut:
   4 corner squares, each 3½" x 3½"
   2 rectangles, each 2" x 3½"
   20 squares, each 3⅞" x 3⅞"; cut once diagonally to yield 40 half-square triangles.
5. Sew background and print half-square triangles together to make 40 squares.
6. Arrange pieced squares and corner squares around the quilt, balancing the colors and rotating the triangles as shown.
7. Join 12 pieced squares to make each side border, trimming the 2 center squares on each side by ¾" to make the correct side lengths. Adjust the amount to be trimmed from the center squares as necessary to fit your quilt.

Adjust border length here.

Sew pieced borders to sides of quilt top.

8. Join 8 pieced squares, 2 corners squares, and a rectangle in the center as shown, to make the top and bottom borders. Adjust the width of the center rectangle to make the correct top and bottom width.

Adjust border length here.

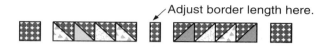

Sew pieced borders to top and bottom of quilt top.

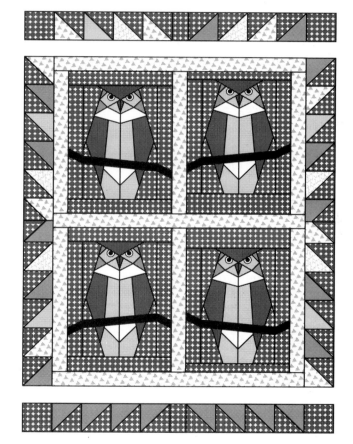

Quilt Finishing

1. Layer the quilt top with batting and backing; baste.
2. Quilt in the design of your choice.
3. Bind the quilt with 2½"-wide, straight-grain strips cut from the black print. You will need approximately 144" of binding.

USING the BIRD and ANIMAL DESIGNS to CREATE QUILTS

This book offers you a set of patchwork designs and some suggestions for quilts using the designs. But I hope that you will use the patterns in quilts of your own design. You may not even want to make quilts! The designs can be used for tote bags, pillows, aprons, Christmas decorations—in fact, in any project in which patchwork can be used.

Playing with the Block Designs

The best approach to creating your own quilts, using the animal designs, is simply to play with the blocks themselves and investigate the possibilities. For creative people, this kind of "play" is serious business. What it means is that you keep asking "what happens if I . . . " and try as many possibilities as you can. Some will not work immediately, but some will, and some may suggest other possibilities. Trace or photocopy one of the smaller representations of the block designs, then make lots of copies, cut them up, and begin to play.

The majority of the animal block designs are asymmetrical, which just means that they have a left and right side and do not have two halves that are identical. The only symmetrical blocks in the collection are the Moose and Swallow blocks; the Moose block divides in half vertically, while the Swallow block divides across the diagonal.

While you are playing, look at both the pattern you create with the animal design itself (called positive space), as well as the pattern that is created by the space around the animal (called negative space). For example, in the Flock of Swallows quilt (page 74), the birds create wonderful shapes in the negative spaces around their wings.

In some of the animal blocks, the edge of the block is also the edge of the animal or bird. These blocks may need "air" space around the animal; otherwise, when the block is repeated, the shapes run into each other. Air space is created by surrounding the block with strips of background fabric. Treat the block plus the extra strips as your unit for making designs.

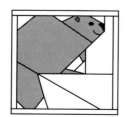

Exploring Repetition

When any of the blocks (or groups of blocks) are repeated, secondary patterns and rhythms develop, which is why repetition is such a powerful tool in quilt design. There are three basic possibilities for repeating the

blocks, although there are many variations of these, as shown on page 91.

The following three possibilities are a good place to begin your creative exploring.

1. Repeat the block as is. This repetition can be done horizontally, vertically, or diagonally. For example, in the Robin in Springtime quilt (page 66), the same Robin block is repeated four times on the diagonal. (See #2 on page 91.)

   The blocks can also be repeated in a stepped pattern. The stepped pattern can be vertical in a brick pattern, as in #4 on page 91; or it can be horizontal in a half-drop pattern, as in #5.
2. Repeat the block as a reverse or mirror image. This reversal can be done horizontally or vertically. See the Tartan Squirrels quilt (page 70).
3. Repeat the block by rotating it around a point. For examples of rotating blocks, see the Flock of Swallows quilt (page 74), the Cardinal quilt (page 44), and the Hummingbird quilt (page 52).

Combining Straight-Line Blocks with Patchwork Blocks and Borders

The possibilities are endless, and the quilts in this book represent only a fraction of them. Following are several ideas.

1. Small wall hangings can be made by surrounding an animal block with one or two borders, with perhaps some very simple piecing added, such as squares in the corners. Some of the animal blocks may need strips of background sewn around them to create air space, before borders are added.
2. Repeat the animal blocks with sashing between them. See the Owl quilt (page 87); to add more interest, some blocks have been reversed and dropped slightly by adding sashing strips of different sizes around each block.
3. Repeat the animal blocks with alternating plain or pieced blocks. In the Moose quilt (page 61), the Moose blocks alternate with nine-patch blocks. See also the Robin in Springtime quilt (page 66).
4. Repeat the blocks with both sashing and alternating pieced blocks between them. In the Blue Jay Chain quilt (page 40), the jays alternate with a five-patch chain block, but there is also sashing between the blocks, with squares (sometimes called "posts") in each corner forming part of the chain.
5. Use a single block (or group of blocks) as the center of a medallion-style quilt and surround the animal(s) with other patchwork blocks and/or borders. The Canada Goose quilt (page 48) is a good example of the use of simple patchwork borders. In the Eagle in the Mountains quilt (page 82), the eagle is positioned in the center of Delectable Mountains blocks.
6. Make the animal block into a picture. See the Honey

Exploring Repetition

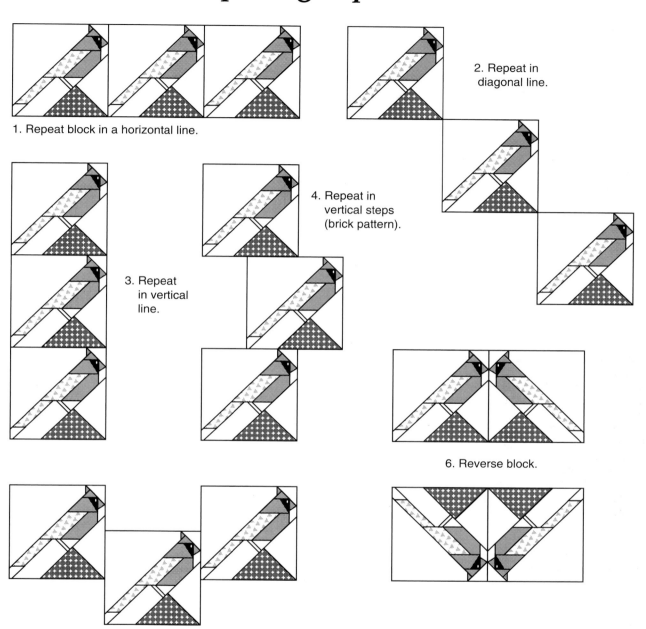

1. Repeat block in a horizontal line.

2. Repeat in diagonal line.

3. Repeat in vertical line.

4. Repeat in vertical steps (brick pattern).

6. Reverse block.

5. Repeat in horizontal steps (half drop).

7. Rotate block around axis.

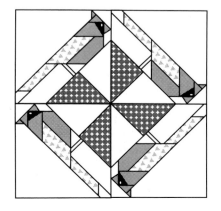

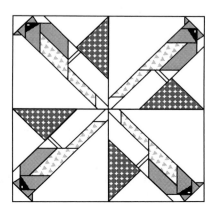

Bear quilt (page 29), where the bear is combined with a tree.

7. Use the animal block with a related traditional block. The Bear's Paw quilt (page 26) combines the Bear's Paw block with Bear blocks; and the Mallard Duck quilt (page 56) combines the Duck block with Duck and Ducklings blocks.

8. Use part of a traditional block to create a border. In the Mallard Duck quilt (page 56), the outside corners of the Duck and Ducklings block are used to frame the Duck block.

9. Feature patchwork borders. See the Owl quilt (page 87) and the Tartan Squirrels quilt (page 70).

10. Piece the sashing. In the Tartan Squirrels quilt (page 70), squares are pieced into the center of the sashing between the squirrels.

11. Combine blocks of different sizes.

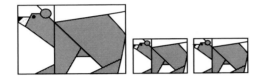

12. Use the animal designs to make a quilt border. See the Bear's Paw quilt (page 26).

13. Rotate the block 45° so that it is on point (so the square becomes a diamond) and combine it with other diagonal patterns. See the Eagle in the Mountains quilt (page 82).

14. Combine the animal blocks together to create a quilt, using several of the animals and/or birds.

Many of the animal blocks are based on a grid of 12 x 12 squares, so they combine well with all blocks divisible by 4 (such as a four-patch) and all blocks divisible by 3 (such as a nine-patch). This is because 12 can be divided by both 3 and 4.

Other blocks, however, are based on a grid of 8 x 8 squares. While they are simple to combine with blocks divisible by 4, they are not simple to combine with blocks divisible by 3.

The easiest way to combine both types of blocks (8 x 8 grid and 12 x 12 grid) is to choose a size that is compatible with blocks divisible by 3 and blocks divisible by 4 (such as 12").

To combine two blocks of incompatible size, you must alter the size of one of the blocks to make them compatible. For example, in the Blue Jay Chain quilt (page 40), the Blue Jay block was made into a 10" square so that it could be combined with a five-patch block. To alter the size of any block, see pages 8–10.

Using Color Creatively

In the color key for each animal block, the natural colors for the animal are suggested. Don't feel confined to making the animal blocks in only natural colors. Be as creative as you like. See the Tartan Squirrels quilt (page 70), for example. Remember, you are making a patch-work quilt, not a real animal.

If you do change the colors (and even if you don't), try to keep the values (lightness and darkness) in the design correct. It is the values that really create the characteristic look of the bird or animal. For example, a raccoon must have dark eye patches, no matter whether he is gray, brown, green, or purple. It is also good to have a difference in value between the animal and the background, so that the animal shape is clear. However, if you want the animal to deliberately blend into the background, use fabrics that are similar in value for the animal and background.

Use prints creatively to suggest textures and to add interest. Change the prints in the blocks to add variety. A good quilt is one that your eyes like to linger over, and a variety of prints can be a delight to the eye. In the Owl quilt (page 87), each owl is made up of a different group of fabrics, although relative values were maintained consistently.

When you are fabric shopping, always be on the lookout for prints that are "just right" for either the animals or for their surroundings. When I wanted to make the Robin in Springtime quilt (page 66), I wanted a fabric that sang "Spring," and I found a particularly lovely floral print. Sometimes a fabric "find" can inspire a quilt. When you find a particular fabric that is appealing, you can create a whole quilt by just working around the colors in one fabric. Use the colors in the print to suggest colors and values of other fabrics that will combine well with your original choice. Be wary, however, of overmatching; it just leads to dullness. Sometimes, you may find a print that will make a great border; in this case, work from the colors in the border print to select the colors you need for the quilt center.

Changing the Size of the Quilts

Any one of the suggested quilts can be made in a different size. There are several ways of doing this.

1. Make more or fewer blocks. For example, the Bear's Paw quilt (page 26) could be made larger by adding six more Bear's Paw blocks, so instead of being three rows of three blocks, it would be five rows of three. The side borders would then need to be cut longer to fit, and two more bears could be added in the border, if you wish. The size of the finished quilt top would be 49½" x 73½".

2. Increase or decrease the size of everything in the quilt. For example, the Bear's Paw quilt is 49½" x 49½", based on a unit of 1½" in which the Bear's Paw blocks are seven-patch blocks of 1½" squares, the sashing and first border are 1½" wide, and the Bear blocks are 6" x 9" (multiples of 1½). By making the unit size 2", the Bear's Paw blocks would be 14" square, the borders 2" wide, and the Bear blocks 8" x 12" (multiples of 2), and the finished size of the quilt top would then be 66" square.

Many of the quilts combine an animal block and a traditional block that are both the same size. See the Robin in Springtime quilt (page 66). Both blocks could be enlarged to make a new size. When you change the size of the blocks, however, the blocks may become less compatible with each other, so one or other of the blocks may have to be drawn following the special directions on pages 8–10.

3. Change the size of the border or borders. This is a very simple way of changing the size of the quilt. Adding extra borders will also make a quilt larger.

Quilting books and magazines are filled with lots of ideas for quilt designs. Two books I would especially recommend are *One-of-a-Kind Quilts* by Judy Hopkins and *Blockbuster Quilts* by Margaret J. Miller.

METRIC CONVERSION

Having grown up with the imperial system in a country that has recently changed to the metric system, I have learned that the important principle in metric conversion is not to exchange imperial measurements into exact metric measurements. The results of doing this are a nightmare, such as ¼" becoming 0.65cm, and 12" becoming 30.48cm. It is better to choose near equivalents that are whole numbers and that are suitable for patchwork, and moreover, suitable for the particular project on which you are working. To be useful for patchwork, you need whole metric numbers that give possibilities of division—What is the point of having a number, such as 41cm, that cannot be divided neatly in any way?

I suggest the following three rules for metric conversion:

1. Whatever you do, don't mix the two systems together. Use one or the other, and stick to it. No equivalents between the systems are ever really exact.

2. Always start your conversion with the size of the block in the quilt. Convert the block size to the nearest metric equivalent which will be suitable for that block. This should be a number that is divisible by the number of "patches" or squares in the block. (See page 16.) For instance, all nine-patch blocks should be converted to sizes divisible by 3 (such as 24cm, 30cm, 36cm); four-patch blocks should be converted to a size divisible by 4 (such as 24cm, 32cm); five-patch blocks should be divisible by 5 (such as 25cm, 30cm); and seven-patch blocks should be divisible by 7 (such as 28cm, 35cm).

For strips, sashings, and borders, work out the equivalent size as a proportion of the block. For example, if the imperial block size is 9" for a nine-patch, and sashing strips are 1½", your metric equivalent would be a 24cm block with 4cm strips.

Note that in the imperial system, 12" is the magic number because it is the block size that you can combine with both nine-patch and four-patch blocks (12 is divisible by 3 and 4). In the metric system, 24cm (which is about 9½") is the magic number that can be combined easily with nine-patch and four-patch blocks because 24 is also divisible by 3 and 4.

3. Use 0.75cm as the width for your seam allowances for machine piecing automatic seam allowances. This is a good size to replace the ¼" seam allowance because it results in convenient measurements for patchwork shapes with automatic seam allowances. So for strips, squares, and rectangles, add 1.5cm to your finished measurements to make automatic seam allowances. For an explanation of how the 0.75cm-wide seam allowance works for triangles with automatic seam allowances, see the diagram below. For half-square triangles, cut a square that is 2.5cm larger than the size of the short sides of the finished triangle, then cut this square once diagonally to yield 2 triangles with 0.75cm-wide seam allowances.

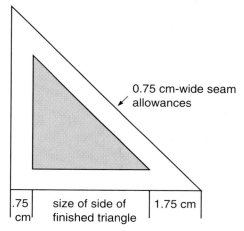

Automatic seam allowances for half-square triangles

0.75 cm-wide seam allowances

.75 cm | size of side of finished triangle | 1.75 cm

= size of side of finished triangle plus 2.5 cm

For quarter-square triangles, cut squares that are 3.5cm larger than the longest side of the triangle, then cut these squares twice diagonally to yield 4 triangles with 0.75cm-wide seam allowances.

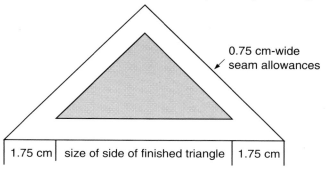

Automatic seam allowances for quarter-square triangles

0.75 cm-wide seam allowances

1.75 cm | size of side of finished triangle | 1.75 cm

= size of side of finished triangle plus 3.5 cm

The numbers for the width of automatic seam allowances should be easy to remember:

1. Add 1.5cm to squares, rectangles, and strips.
2. Add 2.5cm to squares cut for half-square triangles (yield: 2 triangles).
3. Add 3.5cm to squares cut for quarter-square triangles (yield: 4 triangles).

Metric conversion is not a problem for straight–line patchwork blocks, where sewing an exact seam allowance is not a requirement because the sewing line is marked. Seam allowances should be cut about 1cm wide for most pieces and 2cm wide for small or long, pointed pieces. After stitching, these seam allowances can be trimmed to 0.75cm to match the other blocks, sashing strips, borders, and so on.

Table of Useful Metric Equivalents for Patchwork

Note that this table does not give exact equivalents; rather, the numbers have been rounded off to the nearest useful (in terms of patchwork) metric equivalent. Some measurements have alternatives given because it depends on whether the nearby whole metric number is rounded up or down from its imperial equivalent. This choice of numbers gives you the freedom to choose a size that suits the number of patches in the block you are making.

¼" = 0.75cm
½" = 1cm or 1.5cm when you are adding two
    0.75cm seam allowances together
¾" = 2cm
1" = 2.5cm
1¼" = 3cm
1½" = 4cm
2" = 5cm
2½" = 6cm
3" = 8cm
4" = 10cm
5" = 12cm
6" = 15cm
8" = 20cm
9" (¼ yd.) = 24cm
10" = 24cm (for nine- or four-patch blocks)
    or 25cm (for five-patch blocks)
12" = 30cm (for nine- or five-patch blocks)
    or 32cm (for four-patch blocks)
14" = 36cm (for four-patch blocks)
    or 35cm (for seven-patch blocks)
15" = 36cm (for nine-patch blocks)
    or 35cm (for five-patch blocks)
16" = 40cm
18" (½ yd.) = 48cm
20" = 50cm
36" (1 yd.) = 90cm
40" = 100cm

Metric Conversions for Quilts

(finished sizes given)

Honey Bear
Bear block: 16cm x 24cm, 1 square = 2cm
Tree block: 28cm x 16cm, 1 square = 4cm
Inner border: 2.5cm wide
Outer border: 5cm wide

Bear's Paw
Bear blocks: 16cm x 24cm, 1 square = 2cm
Bear's Paw blocks: 28cm x 28cm, seven-patch block,
    1 square = 4cm
Inner border: 4cm wide
Outer border: 16cm wide

Beaver
Beaver block: 32cm x 32cm, 1 square = 4cm
Sashing around Beaver block: 2.75cm wide
Tree blocks: 12.5cm square, 5 x 5 squares,
    1 square = 2.5cm
Outer border: 10cm wide

Eager Beaver
Beaver block: 24cm x 24cm, 1 square = 3cm
Tree blocks: 24cm, 4 x 4 squares, 1 square = 6cm
Inner border: 2cm wide
Outer border: 12cm wide

Blue Jay Chain
Blue Jay block: 30cm block, 1 square = 5cm
Chain block: 30cm, five-patch block, 1 square = 6cm
Sashing strips: 6cm wide
Outer border: 15cm wide

Cardinal
Cardinal block: 24cm block, 1 square = 2cm
Whirligig blocks: 16cm x 16cm, Four–patch block,
    1 square = 4cm
Inner border: 2.5cm wide
Outer border: 10cm wide

Canada Goose
Canada Goose block: 36cm block, 1 square = 3cm
Pieced borders of triangles: 4.5cm squares, 9cm quarter-
    square triangles, and 4.5cm half-square triangles
Sashing: 4.5cm wide
Pieced border of squares: 9cm squares
Outer border: 18cm wide

Mallard Duck
Mallard Duck block: 13.75cm x 30cm block,
    1 square = 2.5 (Omit pieces 20 and 21 when
    making the Mallard Duck quilt.)
Strips at sides of duck: 5cm wide
Strip below duck: 5.25cm wide
Strip above duck: 5cm wide (Mallard Duck block with
    strips added is 24cm x 40cm.)
Pieced strips above and below duck: 8cm x 40cm (8cm
    pieced squares and 8cm x 24cm rectangles) (Com-
    pleted Mallard Duck block with pieced strips added

is 40cm x 40cm.)
Duck and Ducklings block: 40cm, five-patch block,
   1 square = 8cm
Inner border: 4cm wide
Pieced outer border: 32cm quarter-square triangles,
   16cm quarter-square triangles

Hummingbird
Hummingbird block: 32cm, 1 square = 4cm
Pieced border: 16cm wide, with 32cm quarter-square
   triangle set between 2 strips, one 4cm wide and the
   other 12cm wide
Inner border: 4cm wide
Outer border: 16cm wide

Moose
Moose block: 24cm x 24cm, 1 square = 3cm
Nine-patch block: 24cm x 24cm, 1 square = 8cm
Inner border: 6cm wide
Outer border: 12cm wide

Robin in Springtime
Robin block: 24cm x 24cm, 1 square = 2cm
Road to Oklahoma blocks: 24cm x 24cm,
   four-patch block, 1 square = 6cm
Inner border: 4cm wide
Outer border: 12cm wide

Tartan Squirrels
Squirrel blocks: 24cm square, 1 square = 3cm
Pieced sashing between squirrels: 6cm wide
Small Square in a Square blocks: 6cm x 6cm
Inner border: 3cm wide
Large Square in a Square blocks: 12cm x 12cm

Raccoon
Raccoon block: 24cm x 24cm, 1 square = 3cm
Large triangles around raccoon: 24cm quarter-square
   triangles
Pieced triangles: 6cm half-square triangles
Inner border: 3cm wide
Outer border: 6cm wide with pieced corners 6cm x 6cm

Flock of Swallows
Swallow block: 24cm x 24cm, 1 square = 3cm
Flock of Geese block: 24cm square, four-patch block,
   1 square = 6cm
Pieced border: 12cm half-square triangles

Eagle in the Mountains
Eagle block: 32cm x 32cm, 1 square = 4cm
Sashing around Eagle: 4cm wide
Delectable Mountains block: 20cm block, five-patch block,
   1 square = 4cm
Inner border: 4cm wide
Pieced border: 5cm half-square triangles
Outside border: 5cm wide

Owl
Owl block: 32cm x 20cm, 1 square = 4cm
Strips at sides of Owl blocks: 4cm
Strips at top and bottom of Owl blocks: 4cm, 2cm, or
   6cm as appropriate to vary position of bird, to make
   each Owl block 40cm x 28cm
Sashing and inner border: 4cm wide
Pieced outer border: 8cm half-square triangles

Margaret Rolfe, an Australian quiltmaker, has had a lifelong interest in patchwork and quilting. She was particularly inspired to make quilting her own craft after living in the United States for several months in 1975. At that time, the American Bicentennial year was approaching, and quilting was about to be discovered by American women as an exciting craft with a rich and wonderful past and a great creative future. After returning to Australia, Margaret combined the knowledge she had gleaned in the United States with a lot of learning by trial and error to make her own quilts.

During the 1980s Margaret began to create original quilt designs. Her first were quilts of Australian wild flowers and wildlife. She found pieced blocks most intriguing, and her experimentation led to her unique approach to patchwork design and sewing. Her straight-line patchwork technique, as featured in this book, is the result.

Margaret's designs have been published in a series of books, including *Australian Patchwork Designs*, *Quilt a Koala*, and *Patchwork Quilts to Make for Children*. Her interest in history is reflected in her book *Patchwork Quilts in Australia*.

Go Wild with Quilts is the result of Margaret's five-year sojourn in Canada and many trips to the United States, during which she became acquainted with the birds and animals native to these countries. Her quilting career is enthusiastically supported by her scientist husband, Barry, and her three student-aged children, Bernard, Phil, and Melinda. Phil has done illustrative drawings for many of her books, and he contributed the delightful drawings of the animals and birds in this book.